# Looking Back

# Looking Back

Memories of World War II by Residents
of University Retirement Community

Davis, California

*Looking Back*, initially approved by the
URCAD Inreach/Outreach Committee, is
available for sale. The book is a soft cover
publisher's format of 154 pages published
by the I Street Press in Sacramento,
California.

A copy of the book will be exhibited in the
URC Library with order forms.

## Looking Back

Memories of World War II by
Residents of University Retirement
Community, Davis, California

placed in each Resident's mail slot.

Books are available at a price of $14.99 each. Profit of approximately $4.00 per copy from the book beyond the cost of publishing will be donated to the URCAD Foundation and/or other charity to be determined by the Inreach/Outreach Committee.

I _____ Apt _____ would like to order _____ copies of ***Looking Back*** at $14.99 a copy and am enclosing a check for $_____ paid to Patrick Crowley for a revolving fund to print additional books. At lower left on your check enter "WW II Book." Place this completed form with your check in mail slot #1336

# Looking Back

Memories of World War II by Residents of
University Retirement Community
Davis, California

Edited by Patrick Crowley

## Contributing Editors

Joan Callaway
Scott Johnson
Amy Moore
Georgia Paulo
Jasper Schad
Joyce Takahashi
Prescott Williams

I Street Press
Sacramento, California

Crowley, Patrick. Editor
    Looking Back: Memories of World War II / by the Residents of University Retirement Community, Davis, California. Sacramento: I Street Press, 2020.

    ISBN: 978-1-952337-05-5

    Library of Congress Control Number: 2020910392

Book Layout © 2020 BookDesignTemplates.com

Printed in the United States by the I Street Press

First Edition
Second Printing

# Dedication

This book is dedicated to our University Retirement Community Veterans who served during World War II. They constitute the last remaining members of the Greatest Generation who answered the call to save the world from totalitarianism and preserve democracy and the American way of life. With the return of the veterans, we entered a new era of prosperity, growth in personal wealth and openness in our society never previously seen. Clearly, with the winning of the War, the world had changed forever. We also recognize all their family members who supported their effort and waited at home for their return.

# Contents

# In Uniform

# Introduction

The year 2020 marks the 75th anniversary of the end of World War II. In the fall of 2017, I approached the Inreach/Outreach Committee at University Retirement Community here in Davis, California, with the suggestion that we create a book memorializing the efforts of URC residents who participated, either in uniform or as civilians, in that conflict. It has taken until now in May 2020 to complete the project too long delayed by reliance on volunteers and other circumstances to bring this book to completion. Ready to go to press earlier this year, our publisher was shut down by the Coronavirus which has brought our country to a standstill unlike anything since World War II's impact on our economy and the lives of us all.

Among the residents at University Retirement Community are a number of individuals who have a story to tell and have volunteered to have their stories collected in book form. Having the information in a book makes it possible to share it with friends, family, other residents, and others interested in the history of the period.

Among our stories are a number of those of individuals who neither served in the active military nor remained at home. We have residents who were born overseas and others who were interned as Japanese-Americans Still others were witnesses of historic events or served in a different capacity, including one resident who served as a conscientious objector.

With respect to those who served, because of the age of many individuals included in our book, a limited number saw actual combat or served overseas, but they experienced various phases of training in preparation for overseas service. Others served in capacities that released others for overseas duty.

The wide variety of experiences of all of our participants helps illustrate the fact that nearly everyone alive at the time of World War II was affected in one way or another. The world has never been the same in almost every way. Despite the horror and destruction of the War, it was a life-changing experience for the country as well as individuals. Many Americans, even though they had their lives changed forever, might not have ever traveled out of our country and, in many cases, not out of their hometowns and even states were it not for the War.

The conflict brought full economic recovery from a devastating Great Depression that even major social and investment programs by our government had failed to fully address. Full employment in the war effort was responsible for massive internal migration as workers filled defense industry jobs. Women, in many cases for the first time, found employment outside the home as they replaced men in critical jobs. New vistas were opened to women who were able to serve in the military.

There was almost no segment of society that did not benefit one way or the other. With the successful winning of the War, the G. I. Bill enabled returning veterans who might never have considered higher education to fill our colleges and universities. With industry freed from producing war materials, it reverted to producing household products to fill the need for things not produced for civilian consumption during the War. The pent-up demand for consumer products helped create a booming economy. Automobiles were again produced, and there was a huge surge in home construction aided by VA and FHA loans. The impending struggle with Communism was on the horizon, but it was in the background for men and women tired of war and happy to create lives of their own. Significant progress was made in the area of racial equality as more minorities gained important roles in the war effort. Despite the horrendous cost in human lives, huge gains were made in fields of science, medicine, and technology. In retrospect, a major segment of the population truly experienced the American dream for the first time in Post-War America.

The stories in our book illustrate that transition to a new and better time.

Patrick Crowley
30 May 2020

# Chronology of World War II

## Pre-War

1932   *November 8*: President Roosevelt elected President of
the United States.

1934   *August 19*: Hitler declares himself Fuhrer.
*October*: The "Long March" of Chinese Communists
led by Mao Zedong begins.

1936   *July 17*: The Civil War begins in Spain.
*November 1*: President Roosevelt re-elected as President
of the United States.
*November 26*: Anti-Comintern Pact signed by Germany
and Japan against International Communism.

1937   *January 19:* Japan officially withdraws from the 1921
Treaty limiting the size of their navy.
*July 31*: After beginning hostilities with China, Japan
occupies Beijing.
*December 13*: Nanking falls to the Japanese Army:
"Rape of Nanking."

1938   *January 28*: President Roosevelt calls for a massive
rearmament program for the United States.
*March 12*: Germany announces Anschluss (union) with
Austria followed a day later by the annexation of
Austria to the Third Reich.
*September 30*: Hitler and British Prime Minister Neville
Chamberlain meet in Munich, agree to cede

Czechoslovakia's Sudetenland to Germany
Chamberlain claims "peace in our time."
*November 9*: The Kristallnacht pogrom unleashes
widespread attacks on German Jews.

## The War Years

1939   *August 23:* Germany and U.S.S.R. sign non-aggression
pact.
*September 1*: German forces invade Poland; Britain and
France declare war against Germany; the United States
proclaims neutrality.
*October 14*: German U-boat sinks *HMS Royal Oak* at
anchor in Scapa Flow, killing 883.
*November 10*: the Soviet Union invades Finland, the
Winter War begins.

1940   *January 8*: Rationing of butter, sugar, and bacon begins
in Great Britain.
*March 12*: Finland signs a peace treaty with the Soviet
Union.
*May 9*: Germany invades Holland, Belgium, and
Luxemburg.
*May 10*: Chamberlain resigns as Prime Minister;
Winston Churchill is asked to form a new
government.
*May 13*: Churchill makes his "Blood, sweat, tears and
toil" speech to the House of Commons.
*May 26*: Operation Dynamo, the evacuation of British,
French and Belgian troops from Dunkirk begins.
*May 28*: Belgium finally surrenders.
*June 10*: Italy declares war on Britain and France.
*June 14*: German troops enter Paris.
*July 1*: French government of Marshall Petain
established in Vichy.
*July 10*: German air forces begin the Battle of Britain.
*July 23*: the Soviet Union officially absorbs Lithuania,
Latvia, and Estonia.

*August 23*: German air raids on central London begin
*August 25*: First Royal Air Force raid on Berlin.
*September 2*: President Roosevelt agrees to transfer 50
World War I destroyers to Great Britain in exchange
for leases of naval bases in the Western Hemisphere.
*September 16*: The United States enacts peacetime Draft
law.
*October 28*: Italy invades Greece.

1941    *January 22:* Tobruk, Libya falls to British and
Commonwealth forces.
*February 12*: General Rommel and the Afrika Korps
arrive in Libya.
*March 11*: President Roosevelt signs the Lend-Lease
Act.
*June 22*: Germany launches Operation Barbarossa, the
massive invasion of the Soviet Union.
*July 26*: The United States freezes Japanese assets in
the U.S. and suspends diplomatic relations.
*August 14*: Churchill and Roosevelt sign the Atlantic
Charter.
*September 9*: Germans begin 900-day siege of
Leningrad.
*October 2*: German army launches operation on
Moscow.
*October 31:*  Destroyer USS Reuben James sunk by
German U-Boat while escorting merchant convoy to
Great Britain; First U.S. ship sunk in the War with 44
survivors of a crew of 159.
*December 7*: Japanese naval and air forces attack the
United States naval base at Pearl Harbor, Hawaii.
*December 8*: the U.S. declares war on Japan.
*December 10*: Beginning of Japan's invasion of the
Philippines.

1942    *January 5*: Tire rationing begins in the U.S.
*January 16*: Japan invades Burma.

*February 1*: Germany begins mass deportation of Jews from Western Europe to extermination camps in Poland.

*February 15*: British surrender to Japanese forces in Singapore.

*February 19*: President Roosevelt issues executive order authorizing the internment of Japanese-Americans.

*February 27*: Allied naval forces heavily damaged in the Battle of the Java Sea.

*March 9*: Dutch East Indies surrender to Japanese.

*April 18*: Jimmy Doolittle leads B-25 attack on the Japanese home islands launched from the aircraft carrier *USS Hornet*.

*May 4-8*: Battle of the Coral Sea: U.S. Navy turns back Japanese navy advance on Papua-New Guinea and Australia.

*May 15*: the U.S. begins gasoline rationing.

*June 4-7*: the U.S. wins Battle of Midway, sinking four Japanese aircraft carriers.

*July*: U.S. 8th Air Force arrives in Great Britain.

*July 1-27*: Battle of El Alamein in North Africa.

*August 7*: U.S. First Marine Division invades Guadalcanal.

*October 23*: Second Battle of El Alamein begins.

*November 4*: German troops begin a retreat from El Alamein.

*November 8*: Operation Torch: U.S. invasion of North Africa.

1943   *January 10*:  Red Army begins offensive against Germans in Stalingrad.

*January 18*: Jews in Warsaw ghetto begin an uprising against the Nazis

*January 23*: U.S. troops take Tripoli.

*February 1*: Field Marshall Paulus surrenders to Red Army in Stalingrad.

*February 14*: The Battle of the Kasserine Pass in Tunisia begins.

*March 16*: Climax of the Battle of the Atlantic: 27 merchant ships sunk in one week by German U-boats.

*July 9*: The Invasion of Sicily (Operation Husky) begins.

*July 25*: Mussolini is arrested by order of the Italian King, ending Fascist rule.

*September 8*: Italy surrenders unconditionally to Allies; German forces rushed to Italy.

*September 9*: Allied forces land at Salerno and Taranto.

*October 13*: Italy declares war on Germany.

*November 20*: U.S. Marines land in the Gilbert Islands.

*November 28*: Roosevelt, Churchill, and Stalin meet at the Teheran Conference.

*December 12*: Field Marshall Rommel takes over as commander in chief of the French coastal defenses.

*December 24*: General Eisenhower appointed Supreme Allied Commander, Europe.

1944    *January 17*: Allies attack Germans at Monte Cassino, Italy.

*January 22*: U.S. Fifth Army lands at Anzio, 30 miles south of Rome.

*January 27*: Siege of Leningrad lifted at 900 days; 1 million casualties.

*February 1*: U.S. troops begin the fight for Kwajalein, Marshall Islands.

*March 4*: Allies launch the first daylight raid on Berlin.

*May 26*: Charles DeGaulle proclaims his Free French movement to be the provisional government of the French Republic.

*June 4*: Allies enter Rome, first Axis capital to be liberated.

*June 6*: D-Day (Operation Overlord): Allies invade Normandy, France.

*July 4*: Allies have landed some 920,000 troops in France, with more than 62,000 men killed, wounded and missing.

*July 21*: U.S. Marines land on Guam.

*August 8:* the U.S. completes capture of the Marianas Islands

*August 15*: Allies launch Operation Dragoon, invasion of southern France.

*September 3*: British Second Army liberates Brussels.

*September 17*: Allies launch Operation Market Garden in a failed attempt to secure bridges over the Rhine.

*October 14*: Implicated in a plot against Hitler, Rommel commits suicide.

*October 20*: the U.S. begins the invasion of Leyte, Philippines. Three-day naval Battle of Leyte Gulf begins from the 23rd.

*December 16*: Germany launches a counterattack, "The Battle of the Bulge," in the Ardennes Forest.

*December 21*: Germans besiege U.S. paratroopers in Bastogne and capture St. Vith.

*December 21*: Bastogne relieved by the U.S. 4th Armored Division.

1945 *January 9*: U.S. troops land on Luzon, Philippines.

*January 17:* Red Army captures Warsaw.

*February 4*: Roosevelt, Churchill, and Stalin meet at Yalta.

*February 14*: German city of Dresden is firebombed by Allies, killing more than 40,000 civilians.

*February 19*: U.S. Marines begins amphibious assault of Iwo Jima.

*February 23*: The famous flag-raising takes place.

*March 7*: U.S. troops cross the Rhine River at Remagen.

*March 9*: B-29 bombing creates a firestorm in Tokyo, destroying 16 square miles and killing more than 100,000 civilians.

*April 1*: U.S. forces land on Okinawa.

*April 12*: U.S. President Roosevelt dies at Warm Springs, GA.

*April 30*: Hitler commits suicide in his bunker in Berlin.

*May 7*: German general Jodl signs unconditional surrender.

*May 8*: V-E Day (Victory in Europe) proclaimed.

*June 5*: Allies divide Germany into four occupation zones.

*June 18*: President Harry Truman authorizes "Olympic," an invasion plan for Japan scheduled to begin in November.

*July 16*: First U.S. atomic bomb is successfully tested at Alamogordo, New Mexico.

*July 26*: Clement Atlee is elected Prime Minister of Great Britain, replacing Churchill.

*August 6*: U.S. drops atomic bomb on Japanese city of Hiroshima, killing some 140,000 people.

*August 8*: Soviet Union declares war on Japan and invades Manchuria.

*August 9*: U.S. drops a second atomic bomb on Nagasaki, killing some 80,000 people.

*August 14*: Japan surrenders.

*September 2*: Japanese sign surrender agreement aboard the U.S.S. Missouri in Tokyo Bay, officially ending the war.

*September 2*: V-J Day (Victory over Japan) proclaimed.

# In Uniform

# High Finance

## Howard Adler

When a student at Berkeley High School in Berkeley, California, in the 1940's I tried to join the Navy V-12 program and the Army A-12 program. I easily passed the academic requirements but was rejected by both programs because of very poor eyesight. After a physical, the Draft Board classified me as 4F again because of the poor eyesight. After high school graduation in 1944, I began my studies at the University of  California at Berkeley, majoring in Chemical Engineering. I completed 1½ years toward my B.S. degree and participated in the required ROTC program. In September 1945 the Draft Board again contacted me and informed me that I was accepted into "limited service" not to include carrying any firearms. I was sent to Camp Beale in Marysville, California, and with no basic training in the field and was assigned to the Finance Department. I received special training at finance school at Camp Beale. After the Army's financial training, I was assigned permanently to the Finance Department at the Camp Beale Separation Center, a major Army separation center on the U.S. west coast.

One of my duties with two others from the department was to regularly go to the bank in Marysville to pick up $500,000 to $700,000 in cash, all in $20s from the Federal Reserve Bank in San Francisco to disburse to the separating Army personnel processing through Camp Beale. For security on this job, I was issued a 1919 Colt 45 pistol that had no safety feature and was never loaded (World War I Army surplus). I strapped on this "weapon" for the bank trips. The most cash that one person could carry due to its weight was $200,000, always in $20s. No bills larger than $20s were used for separation payments. Besides two others and I from the Camp Beale Finance Department, military police accompanied them on the bank trips. Separation payments were made in cash. Later I sent bonus checks to Air Corp Reserve officers in amounts of as much as $3,000 to $4,000, $500 dollars for each year served.

I continued to serve in this duty until December 1946 when Congress decreed that all draftees had to be discharged. I was one of the last to be released since my job was handling separation-payments to others. I was offered the opportunity to continue working the same job by the Civil Service Commission. I rejected the offer and resumed my studies at Berkeley using the G.I Bill. My Army training and service time provided enough units to qualify me for a minor in Accounting with my Chemical Engineering B.S. degree.

I found humor in my time in military service. While at Camp Beale, I witnessed many court-martial proceedings. On this particular occasion, the defendant was anxious to leave military service and was known for his many antics toward that goal. This episode involved a barracks inspection by the Company Commander. The Sergeant stationed at the barracks entrance loudly declared "attention" as the Inspectors strode officially into the room. As this special inspection continued, our Private stationed himself at the door to the latrine. He too called out loudly "attention" as he pulled a cord that caused all the toilet seats to arise, standing at attention in unison to welcome the Inspecting Officers. Had it been up to me, the young prankster private would have been promoted. However, the Army brass did not find the incident humorous, hence the court-martial proceedings. The private was fined several month's pay, and he did leave the military with a "discharge without honor." I had to collect the fine. Many people did find the prank funny. Somehow the same incident was featured in the popular "No Time for Sergeants," an Andy Griffith Broadway and movie triumph described as a funny military comedy.

Another humorous experience while in finance at Camp Beale that I enjoy recalling happened like this. The three finance workers had returned from a Marysville bank trip. On the table in front of them were huge stacks of $20 bills and the 1919 pistol as they re-counted the money to be sure they had received the correct total of $500,000. A group of new recruits with mops and brooms were sent to clean the interior. They entered by way of a back door and didn't realize they were in the Finance Department. My cohorts and I quickly dealt cards and pretended to be deep in a serious game of poker – obviously with very high stakes. To this day in my mind's eye, I can see and enjoy the incredulous expressions on the faces of those raw recruits. And imagine the stories that those soldiers can tell!

After graduation from Berkeley, I went to St. Louis, Missouri, to work for an uncle at Dykem Company. In St. Louis I met my love, Barbara. We married in 1951 and moved to the San Francisco area in 1953, a return to my roots and a new experience for the St. Louis-reared Barbara. I retired from the Crown Zellerbach Corporation's Flexible Packaging division in 1983 after assignments in various technical and General Management positions over a 30-year period.

*After retirement, my wife Barbara and I moved to Danville for another 28 years. There I was involved in organizing and overseeing the operation of a special police force. In 2012, we relocated to URC where we would be near our three daughters in the Sacramento area. One daughter is the Medical Librarian at the Shriner's Hospital for Children in Sacramento and is a grandmother; another is a physical therapist in Sacramento and the third is a retired owner in the computer service industry and assists me in further development and management of the real estate portfolio.*

# Preparing for Operation Olympic

## Fred Anderson

I was born on July 14, 1923, the youngest of 5 children to a farming family in eastern Nebraska (practically a suburb of Lincoln, the capital of the state.)

My mother died when I was just over a year old, and I was raised by my stepmother from the time I was 2.

I grew up during the roughest part of both the depression and the drought with little extra other than enough to eat, the love of family, and the strong push by my stepmother that we should all get a college education. The net result was that three of my elders finished college, and I was in my second year at Nebraska Wesleyan (a small liberal arts college in Lincoln) at the time of the start of World War II.

I was home for the weekend from college on Sunday approximately at noon when we heard the news on the radio. Frankly, it didn't even occur to me that my life would be so changed by this event. I was not the rebellious type, and the thought of enlisting immediately was scotched by my parent's strong desire that I finish College before enlisting.

Any thoughts I had of deciding what to do was modified by the dawning recognition that my draft number was coming up, and I had to make a decision. As a result, one year later I enlisted in the Navy Reserve. With this action, I was able to complete a third year of College before being called to active duty on July 1, 1943.

The first six months of active duty was spent in a small college in eastern Nebraska and later in Newport News Virginia in what amounted to a holding area waiting for space to be available at Columbia University (NYC) for formal Midshipman training.

I graduated from Columbia in April of 1944 and was commissioned as a Lieutenant (JG). My first assignment (because of my Science Major in College) was to Radar School to learn all about how to handle this new gadget. This took essentially one full year with the time divided between Harvard and MIT.

Almost exactly one year later, I was assigned to a new ship being built in Rhode Island, and my training days were over. Recognize that I had never been near the ocean my entire life.

After a small amount of local training, we were sent to the west coast (San Diego). This required us to transit the Panama Canal. After a short period, we were directed to Pearl Harbor. At this point, the reality of the war started to sink in. When we first arrived in Pearl Harbor, there were only a few ships in sight.

It was now the middle of August. There were enough ships in the harbor that you thought you could walk from one to another around the harbor without touching water at any point. The plan I had received assumed the start of the invasion of Japan in November with our ship scheduled to land on the fifth day of the invasion with a – can you believe this – tire repair outfit that we would pick up in the Philippines.

When the war ended, we were out of the Harbor on a training mission. We were well informed when the news came out. The Harbor was completely lit up with flares from every ship as well as a stern message from headquarters. "This is the Commandant, stop all release of flares."

Needless to say, it was one of the happy days of my life.

After the war, we were first sent to the Philippines to pick up the tire repair outfitted mentioned earlier. I have lost track of time, but we ended up back in Japan in essentially the same location as the invasion plans had indicated. Very quiet there.

Items of interest included small open markets with Japanese selling their family possessions for anyone to provide some sort of American money. A more interesting incident occurred when a few of the ship's younger officers ducked under the markings pointing where we shouldn't go and wandered into the local village. We were watching a small group of Japanese trying to catch fish in a local creek. One of them came over and starting talking to us with an almost perfect "Midwest" accent. He had spent some time in the States and his message was "I told those idiots that our little island would be overwhelmed by the American power."

Our subsequent assignments were first bringing a boatload of troops back to the states from Japan and an additional abortive trip to bring another contingent which was aborted due to bad fuel. With that, we were sent again through the Panama Canal and up the Hudson River for decommissioning of the ship.

Back home in early July. My parents were perfectly happy to have me reenter life, forgetting the three years I was in the service. To me, that was not the thing to do. I applied and was accepted at Stanford in September of 1946 and received my degree in the fall of 1947. My selection of Stanford was simply that it was a beautiful campus and they accepted me.

The military experience was certainly important in determining my career as I stayed in the general area of endeavor including major Government contracts for my entire working career.

I married Lillian MacGregor in 1949. Our marriage lasted until her death in October of 2007 just short of 58 years. We had no children. Subsequently, I married Dorothy Nelson, a fellow resident that I met here.

*My career of 33 years was spent living in the St. Louis area working for a number of companies without moving. After I retired in 1980, my wife and I moved to California where I became a consultant and an associate for a number of small companies. In 2000 my wife and I moved to URC where I was very active as President of the Resident Council twice. In 2007 Lillian died after a serious accident. Subsequently, I married Dorothy Nelson.*

# From Air Corps to Engineers

## Don Brush

That day came on March 7, 1943. At that time the Army Air Corps needed more meteorologists, and people with the needed backgrounds in math and physics were in short supply. Because I had been a math major in college, I was to be sent to an Air Corps Pre-Meteorology Program at Kenyon College in Ohio. The program was not yet open, however. My first twenty years were spent in Birmingham, Alabama. I was born  there in 1923 and began college there as the first in the family to go to college. On Sunday, December 7, 1941, a group of us teenagers were waiting on the lawn of a local church for an afternoon meeting to begin when a late arrival told us the Japanese had bombed Pearl Harbor. We wondered idly whether someday we'd get into it. and for the first few months, I was a "casual" (someone awaiting transfer) at Keesler Field in Biloxi, Mississippi. As casuals we did a lot of marching, were sent to an occasional training film in the post theater, and sometimes did "KP" (washed pots and pans) in the post kitchen. We also learned that if you were with a group of casuals and answered yes to the question "Can anyone here type?" you'd be selected for a small work detail that had nothing to do with typing.

When the program finally opened, I was sent to Kenyon. The program turned out to consist of two semesters of math and physics for a class of about 40 military students. When we finished the program, the Air Corps no longer needed us, however, and we all were sent as casuals to the campus of Ohio State University. There we were housed in the otherwise-empty OSU stadium and did a lot of marching on the football field.

Eventually we were reassigned individually. One of us was sent to the atomic bomb research program at Oak Ridge, Tennessee. Some of us were sent to the infantry and later were in the Battle of the Bulge in Europe. I was sent to Fort Belvoir, Virginia for basic training in the Corps of Engineers. It was during an after-hours visit to the PX (store) while in basic that I heard about D-Day. Basic training was followed by 17 weeks in OCS (Officer Candidate School). Then, on December 12, 1944, I was commissioned a Second Lieutenant in the Corps of Engineers. Before leaving Belvoir I was sent to a month-long Officers' Mechanical Equipment Course on the operation and maintenance of "heavy equipment" (D-8 tractors (called bulldozers or cats, for Caterpillars), scrapers, graders, etc).

My first assignment as a new lieutenant was to take a group through three months of engineering basic training at Fort Lewis, Washington. Winter is not the best time of year for outdoor field exercises at wet Fort Lewis. From there I went to Camp Beale (now Beale AFB) near Marysville (my first time in California) for a week of preparation for shipment overseas. I learned that my destination was to be the island of Luzon in the Philippines and that the Japanese already had been driven out of the area. On May 3 a busload of us were sent from Beale to San Francisco. (I'm told that in those days we had to have passed through the little town of Davis.) We boarded ship that afternoon and left for Manila.

Our ship was not part of a convoy and, to avoid Japanese submarines, we were sent far south of the equator and then back north of it. It took us 23 uneventful days to get to Manila. The war in Europe ended while we were en route. Because all the docks had been destroyed, we went ashore by clambering down a cargo net on the side of the ship and into the same kind of landing craft as those used on D-Day. When the craft hit the beach the front came down and we walked ashore. Our greeting was quite different from the one the Allied troops encountered on the Normandy coast on D-Day. Instead of German defenders, we were confronted by little Filipino boys who wanted to exchange pineapples for cigarettes. Parts of Manila, especially the section called Intramuros, were in ruins. Some of us walked through downtown Manila a little later and saw the destruction up close.

The first weeks in the Philippines were spent as a casual at a Replacement Depot. Then, at last, I was sent to an engineering construction battalion. The battalion was located in a rural area near Nichols Field, a large military airfield south of Manila. The battalion had been operating in the area for several months. Military formalities such as morning formations for rollcall were ignored. We slept and ate in temporary, canvass-covered structures. In the rainy season, narrow strips of aircraft landing mat were put down between tents to avoid walking in mud.

There were four companies in the battalion, and each company had platoons. I was platoon leader of the heavy equipment platoon. I was blessed to have a sergeant whom I admired and who knew more about what we were doing than I did. Our platoon was responsible for the operation and maintenance of the battalion's cats, scrapers, and graders. Some of the maintenance was done in the battalion area and some at the battalion's work sites. We had a truck that regularly made the rounds of the worksites with, for example, drums of diesel fuel. The battalion built new dirt roads and maintained existing dirt roads over a large rural area near Nichols Field. The day the atom bomb was dropped on Hiroshima found us busy extracting a cat (bulldozer) that was mired in mud four feet deep.

Later I was moved to a construction battalion that operated in the same area near Nichols Field but was located on Taft Avenue in the southern part of Manila. By then better facilities had become available in the city. There was even running water. I was company commander of the company that included the heavy equipment platoon. The company had a fleet of trucks for hauling dirt and other construction materials, and we used a large number of Filipino drivers. Among other services, the company supplied all of the construction equipment for the battalion's operations and all of the equipment operators/drivers. The battalion's operations included maintenance of dirt roads, earthwork for a new railroad that was to bring in supplies and equipment, and construction of the foundations for large airplane hangars on Nichols Field. The work generally went well and I enjoyed it. One time we put one of the concrete footings for a hangar in the wrong place, but we poured another one beside it in the right place.

By the end of my stay on Luzon much of Manila had been restored. In drives along Taft Avenue and Dewey Boulevard in the southern part of the city, I saw little remaining evidence of damage from the war. There was even a tennis tournament in the city at the reopened Rizal Stadium. After 14 months on Luzon I was sent back through San Francisco to Ft. Sam Houston in Texas and was discharged on August 2, 1946. On December 7, 1941, I had wondered whether someday I'd get into it. I did, but only the tail end of it.

*With the GI Bill I went to the University of Illinois and completed undergraduate and graduate degrees in engineering. I met my wife, Ann, at Illinois. Prior to appointment as Professor of Engineering at UC Davis in 1964, I was a Senior Staff Scientist with Lockheed Missiles and Space Company's research labs in Palo Alto. Ann and I have three kids, one of whom lives in the region. Ann and I retired from UC Davis in 1993 and moved to URC in 2003.*

# War-Delayed Date

## Dolly Clark

Half a continent apart, two teenagers, still in high school, heard the news on Sunday, December 7, 1941, that Japan had attacked Pearl Harbor. At that time Richard Clark lived in Southern California, in Santa Paula, which lies along the Santa Clara River, a bit inland from Ventura. Surrounded by citrus and avocado groves, the town was also an early center of Southern  California's petroleum industry. Dick's father was a family doctor. Dick was not quite 17 when the war broke out, too young to be called to military service. But he did his bit by participating in patrols of nearby beaches and mountains in search of Japanese who might have been put ashore by submarines. That fear was real, as shortly after the attack on Pearl Harbor, a Japanese midget submarine lobbed some 16 shells onto a nearby oil field, triggering an invasion panic.

Meanwhile, I, Alleine Bubb, or Dolly as everyone called me, was in El Paso. I had spent my early years in a mining town in southern Colorado, where my father, a mining engineer, was in charge. The company closed that mine and reassigned my father to a new one that had opened another, in northern Mexico not far from El Paso. The family moved to that west Texas community, where we lived while my father commuted across the border. I heard the news where I had gone with a young man who had just enlisted in the Army.

Dick and I remained in our respective communities until we graduated from high school, at which point we both went on to college at Stanford. It was soon thereafter that we met. I first took note of Dick in my biology class, where he was assisting the professor with frog dissection. Interested in getting to know him better, I made it a point to seek him out at a student mixer, known as a Jolly-Up. We danced and afterward he walked me back to my dormitory, where he invited me to dinner and a movie the following week.

That date never materialized. In fact, the two of us did not see each other for another three years. He called to report that having just turned 18, he had enlisted in the Army Air Corps. He was excited to have been accepted into the flight training program, as he had earlier developed a strong interest in flying. Santa Paula had an airport, and he had spent quite a bit of time there watching the local ranchers fly in and out. The prospect of becoming a military pilot would fulfill his dream, and he was assigned to a training cohort.

But his anticipation soon turned to disappointment, as even in 1943, the tide was turning, and the prospect of victory over the Axis powers was increasingly likely. Perhaps the Army would not need as many pilots. Certainly, no effort was made to rush him through his training. Nor was the Army interested in explaining what was going on. His group and he were thus kept in the dark and shuttled through eight bases in the South and Southwest, where the men did little beyond menial chores that included peeling a lot of potatoes. He eventually graduated from pre-flight school, but not until much later -VJ Day in August 1945, to be precise. With the war coming to a close, he was never sent on to complete my training.

In the meantime, I pursued my degree at Stanford. But Stanford had become a very different place; the War had changed everything. Most male students and even a number of faculty members were off serving the country. Not only did that put a damper on social life, but it also reduced the number of classes. Blackouts and air raid drills were a regular part of campus life. Women stepped into leadership roles at all levels, including electing the university's first female student body president.

Everyone was encouraged to contribute in some way to the war effort. Some served as hospital aides, rolled bandages or worked at jobs in the community. An acute shortage of field hands to harvest local crops drew a number of Stanford coeds. I pitched in as best I could. I tried knitting blankets, but that was not my forte. I took on odd jobs here and there, as needed, and picked fruit in the nearby Santa Clara Valley orchards.

During vacation periods, I, along with some of my classmates, rode the train back home to El Paso. We rode first class, in compartments, which was unusual given that trains were usually filled with servicemen and women, and civilians had low priority. While getting tickets was not easy, I was in luck. The steam trains of that era used coal, which my father's company supplied to the railroad. That made it much easier for him to get tickets for my friends and me.

But there were other concerns. Most of the passengers were servicemen, and my protective mother, worried about my safety, cautioned me to be extra careful. My mother apparently also intervened to shield me in yet another way. I never heard from Dick during his time in the Air Corps. He professed to have tried to get in touch with me by contacting my mother, but she was not comfortable giving out my address to someone she did not know and trust.

When Dick finally returned to civilian life in November 1945, he headed back to Stanford to pick up where he had left off and resumed his pre-med studies. We soon ran into each other at a student beach party. Although we began spending time together, I soon graduated and returned home to El Paso.

At a time when the whole idea of a college education for young women seemed frivolous to many and career opportunities were few, it was time to face the reality that however much I enjoyed my Latin American Studies program at Stanford, it offered me no future. Looking at my situation from a practical perspective, my parents decided to send me off to New York City to attend an "elite" secretarial school.

Upon graduation nine months later, several other classmates and I set off across the country to San Francisco. Although that seemed an adventurous thing for young women, I was mindful of the fact that Dick was nearby. When my friends and I took up residence in one of the city's guest houses in Pacific Heights and found jobs, Dick and I reconnected, but the demands of his pre-med program left little time for a social life. To see him, I had to travel down to Palo Alto. Things got easier when Dick moved up to San Francisco to complete his training at Stanford Hospital. And before long we married

*After graduating from medical school, Dick went on to an internship in Rochester, New York, followed by two residencies at Highland Hospital in Oakland. In 1955, we moved to Napa, where he set up practice as a family doctor, and we raised four children. By 1976, we felt that it was time to move on, so he accepted an offer of an appointment to the newly established medical school at UC Davis. But he was never really comfortable in academe. Preferring direct contact with patients, he switched courses again, concluding his career at the UC Davis Student Health Center. We were both interested in travel and gardening. We also were active in the local Episcopal Church. In 2008 we moved to URC.*

# 90 Day Wonder

## Romeo Favreau

I trace my family back to 17th century France prior to their immigration to Canada, and then to the United States. I was born on September 29, 1925, in Lowell, Massachusetts; my parents had recently attended a performance of "Romeo and Juliet" and decided that their baby would be named after one of the title characters. I attended Immaculate Conception Catholic School and Lowell High School where I was a Lieutenant in the ROTC. Among my hobbies were rubber band powered model airplane building and the ham radio, license W1PAT.

In September 1942, I entered the Massachusetts Institute of Technology, Cambridge, Massachusetts, first on a partial scholarship and later in the Navy V12 program's full scholarship. Two and a half years later, in June 1945, I received my degree in Physics, and I moved on to Midshipman School at Fort Schuyler New York, New York. There I studied Seamanship, Navigation, Ordnance, Ship Handling, Engineering, and Damage Control and Aircraft Recognition before receiving my officer's commission; I was one of the "ninety-day wonders." On VJ day, August 14, 1945, I was given the day off and found my way to Time Square to celebrate. The major question in my mind was, "What is the Navy going to do with us now?"

Graduating in the class of "November 1945" I was commissioned Ensign. For the next two months, I served in the office of the 1st Naval District Administration, whose responsibility it was to keep an inventory of all Navy vessels along the eastern shorelines of New England. Among those vessels were large pleasure boats, which had been loaned to the navy, and the 50 destroyers, which had been lend-leased to Britain.

My next assignment was to a top-secret Combat Information Center (CIC) on Saint Simon Island, Georgia, where the navy practiced directing aircraft to intercept the enemy. It was like a video game. This location was close enough to Miami, where my mother was living, and I was able to get free flights to visit my mother.

About midway into this assignment, I was given the choice of joining "the fleet" or completing the CIC training and signing up for an additional year of service. Choosing the former, I was ordered to report to a Landing Craft Support (LCS) ship in Little Creek, Virginia, which was equipped with many guns designed to support an infantry landing on enemy shores. The ship had a crew of 35. I was a junior officer in charge of radio transmissions, the gunnery, and the commissary. Radio and gunnery were familiar to me, but as commissary officer, I was charged with acquiring, preparing and serving food for officers and the crew. I was totally inexperienced with anything to do with the handling of food. Even without a "cook," I found that I could rely on the "mess boys" to plan and prepare successful meals.

On discharge, June 30, 1946, I joined Raytheon, the electronics firm in Waltham, Massachusetts, to work on air to air missiles. Several months later, I joined Hughes Aircraft in Culver City, California, where I headed the analog computer lab. On August 1, 1947, Irene Berube from Salem, Massachusetts and I were married.

Hughes Aircraft had grown from a workforce of 35 in 1947 to 2000 in 1954, the year I moved to Electronics Associates in Princeton, New Jersey, as director of the Princeton Computational Center. In 1969 I moved to San

Diego to work for Dillingham Corporation. In 1975 I earned a master's degree in aerospace engineering from UC San Diego and launched my own engineering and consulting firm. I retired in 1992 and moved to Davis with my wife, Irene to be closer to our five children.

*Since I was a pioneer in computer simulation, I volunteered in retirement to manage databases and develop computer models for row crops and river systems with research groups at the University of California, Davis. The UC Davis College of Agricultural and Environmental Science honored me in 2012 for my many years of volunteer service to UCD helping scientists develop computer models.*

*I was involved in many community volunteer efforts, such as Meals on Wheels and the Davis Senior Center, and served as president of the Davis Kiwanis Club*

# Serving in France and Germany

## Noble Keddie

A third-generation Californian, I was born in Stockton, California, in 1925. I graduated six months early from Stockton High School in 1942 in order to join the U. S. armed services. In WW I my father had been a Sergeant in the army and had been awarded the Purple Heart when it was instituted in 1932.

For 3 months of basic training, I was assigned to Camp Roberts, California, 12 miles north of Paso Robles on Highway 101, one of the largest replacement centers for infantry, artillery and armor divisions. I was one of fifty in my platoon, housed in one of the two-storied barracks. Here I trained as a "forward observer," after which I was sent to Mississippi and to Camp Gordon, Alabama, for infantry training.

In early 1945, I was one of 15,000 men on a Queen Mary voyage, which crossed the Atlantic to Northern Scotland in 5 days at a speed to allow them to "out-run" the submarines. Two friends and I were assigned an inside cabin and were served two meals a day in the "mess hall" which was located on top of the wooden cover of the drained swimming pool. After landing, we waited two days and traveled by night on trains to the port in southern England, during which time our rations were issued in square boxes about the size of cigarette cartons. The following night, we climbed aboard a ship to cross to Omaha Beach in Southern France. Only nine months earlier that had been a landing beach for D-Day.

We were transferred by truck to boxcars on an overnight train to Northern France where there was a replacement depot for the Battle of the Bulge. (The Battle had been from 12/16/44 to 1/25/45.) At this point, rifles were issued. In addition, each soldier had to fire 2 grenades into a pit as a preliminary for the standard practice of throwing a grenade before entering a room. I was assigned to a half-track armored personnel carrier. At one point, I was pulled out and taken back 10 miles to a German supply depot, which had been captured and was still full of weaponry. I collected a souvenir or two. On the road, I spotted slaughtered horses and wagons but no retreating German soldiers.

We went through Belgium and arrived at Trier, Germany, where we liberated champagne from an 11-story underground winery. At another city, we arrived after dark, whereupon I was assigned to guard duty. The next morning jet planes strafed them.

In March 1945, the Americans had saved the Ludendorff Bridge, a railroad bridge across the Rhine at Remagen. It was the last remaining bridge across the river. I fired 4 rounds on the bridge as the firing came to a close. (The weakened bridge lasted for only about 12 more days, but it was key to the Allied victory.)

Continuing our search for hidden German soldiers, I traveled in a self-propelled vehicle, which stopped three times a day en route to Switzerland. On V-E Day (May 8, 1945) we were in Garmisch-Partenkirchen, Germany. Between V-E Day and V-J Day, I was assigned to the 20th Division Artillery.

I recalled meeting an African American Armored Division composed of men whose time in service should have led to their discharge, but who were passed over. I also mentioned that two of our officers were Japanese-Americans from Hawaii.

At the end of WWII in Europe, while still in the service, I (still Private Keddie) attended an eight-week term at the G. I. University in the French resort town of Biarritz. The U.S. Army had converted the hotels and casinos into quarters, class and lab spaces for demobilized American servicemen. Typing, chemistry and motion picture production were some of the offerings.

Following my discharge on June 2, 1946, I attended Delta Community College and College of Pacific on California State scholarships, and UCSF School of Dentistry on the GI Bill, graduating in 1953. After about 10 years in private practice, I began doing dentistry with the State of California Department of Corrections at Duell Vocational Institute in Tracy, primarily working on the teeth of juvenile offenders before they were sent out to work in forestry camps. I retired in 1988, and in 2011 I reluctantly revisited Normandy, after which I was glad I did.

*I met Evelyn Lowry on a blind date. (Evelyn confessed to sitting incognito in my waiting room to look me over before agreeing to the date.) We were married in 1957. Since my wife Evelyn is a third-generation Californian, our two daughters are fourth-generation Californians.*

*Our daughter Elise lives in Woodland and Beth in San Rafael. Beth and her husband have two sons. We visited a number of CCRC's before spending a couple of days at URC. We moved to URC in August 2013.*

# Naval Intelligence in Washington, D.C.

## Lewis Mullen

I was born in Forest Park, Illinois, in 1918 and was the oldest of three children. I attended elementary school in Forest Park and then Proviso High School in Maywood, graduating in 1936. After graduation, I worked "any job that paid money" until I had saved enough to enter DePaul University night school in 1938 to study accounting.

I volunteered for the U.S. Navy Reserve in 1941 as I had an interest in the sea gained from books that I had read. I also did not want to be drafted into the infantry. I was called to active duty on October 12, 1941, and was assigned directly to a Naval Intelligence Unit without having gone through the usual "boot camp." I was sent to Great Lakes Naval Training Center near Chicago and issued my uniforms and sea bag.

I was in a USO facility in Kansas City, Missouri, when I heard of the attack on Pearl Harbor on December 7, 1941. I soon received orders transferring me to the Department of the Navy Headquarters in Washington, D.C., assigned to the Intelligence Office photo laboratory. Since I knew nothing about photography, I had to be a "quick learner" in how to develop film and produce printing plates for making copies of photos.

I never have worked so hard in my life often working three straight shifts on work that I could not talk about. Fortunately, the ratio of women to men was approximately 8-

1, so I was surrounded by a group of very hard-working women. It is my opinion that if the USA won the war, it would be due to the efforts of these women.

It was through my assignment at Naval Headquarters that I met Regina Rodman. I had been invited to attend the wedding of a friend and was introduced to Regina, who also worked at Naval Headquarters. We would marry in 1944.

I remember seeing both Presidents Roosevelt and Truman. On one occasion, I was with a group of servicemen and civilians standing in a park watching President Roosevelt being driven by in a parade. When the President saw the group waving, he instructed his driver to pull over to where the group was standing and took the time to shake our hands and greet us all before returning to the parade.

On other occasions, after the death of Roosevelt in April 1945, I would see President Harry Truman on one of his morning walks followed by his two secret service guards. I would yell out "Hi, Mr. President," and Truman would respond "Hi Boys" as he continued his walk. I would spend my entire military assignment in Washington, D.C., before being discharged in December 1945.

After my discharge, Regina and I and our first daughter (also named Regina) moved back to Illinois. Using my G.I. Bill benefits, I again enrolled in night school with an interest in English Literature. I did not graduate, as I had to quit school to find a job to support my family.

I was hired as Administrative Assistant to General Manager of Harding Williams Company, an industrial food supply company providing meals to office buildings and factory employees. I worked at Harding Williams until 1969 when the company was purchased by a larger food service company, Saga Corporation, with headquarters in Menlo Park, California.

I was transferred to Palo Alto, California, as Administrative Assistant to General Manager, tasked with analysis of potential contracts for expanding their foodservice business.

I retired from Saga Corporation in 1985.

After my retirement, I registered at community college and studied biology. I eventually took up "Bonsai," the Japanese art of cultivating trees in small containers, as a hobby.

*Regina and I, having raised two sons and two daughters, began looking for a retirement community to move to and attended a presentation by Pacific Retirement Services where we learned that PRS was planning to build a new facility in Davis, California, to be available in 2000. We signed up and were probably the third family to move into a garden apartment when URC opened in 2000. Regina died in 2012.*

# Trained for the Desert, Sent to Alaska

## Verne Mendel

I was born Verne Mendel April 28, 1923, in Lewistown, Montana, but grew up 45 miles north of there in a village called Winifred. Presumably, Winifred was named after the daughter of a Milwaukee railroad official. These small western towns were spaced 20 miles apart by the railroad because that is how far one could travel in a horse-drawn wagon in one day. Winifred is in the center of a large land area, and the kids from that region went to school in Winifred. I attended school there from 1st to 12th grades.

My father migrated from Wisconsin to Montana because the land was opened to homesteading in that area. My grandfather had never owned land and wanted very much to have some in the family. So in 1910, my father filed for a homestead, which he was given three miles east of the future town of Winifred. It was poor farmland so it has since been given back to the Federal Government.

At age 18 I had never been out of the Lewiston-to-Winifred corridor, so I knew nothing about cities or how they worked until I left for college at Montana State College in Bozeman. My parents had no money to help me, so I had to work to survive. I had not learned how to study and barely survived my freshman year at MSC.

I was living in a boarding house with seven other guys, and one Sunday after lunch we were visiting with the radio turned on, and we were stunned to hear that the Japanese had bombed Pearl Harbor. What to do now was the question on everybody's mind. After several months of thinking about the question, I decided to go to Vancouver, Washington, where I went to work making Liberty ships. I was taught how to weld so I worked as a welder through the winter of 1942. I had significant hearing loss during those months

I was eligible for the Draft and had tried to volunteer in the Horse Cavalry, but it had been changed to a mechanized outfit. I was not interested. One day I received the Draft notice to report the next morning to the Draft Board in Lewistown, Montana, which was impossible to do. Consequently, I was drafted at Vancouver and went into the Army March 1943. After passing the physical exam, I was asked which branch I wanted to go into. I didn't have a clue, so they said, "You will be in the Infantry." I was shipped to Fort Lewis, Washington. I was only there for a few days and was transferred to Camp Roberts, California. We got into Camp Roberts pretty late at night and were shown a barracks and told to go to bed without bedding The next morning the company sergeant came and told us where to get bedding and to make our beds. Shortly after that this guy in the barracks came over, sat on my newly made bed and asked if I was a "damned Yankee." I was so naive that I didn't know what to say. I mumbled something about being a westerner. Then I learned this guy was from Texas, and he was still fighting the Civil War. I soon got tired of hearing this.

Rommel was fighting in the Sahara Desert at the time, so I was trained in Desert Combat. Before the training was completed, Rommel was defeated. One day during training I was told to leave the area and report to a specific building in Camp. When I arrived, I entered a room with several officers seated around a table. I was asked why I wanted to go to Officers Training School. I was asked whether I thought I could do more for my country as a private or as an officer. I said I didn't know, so I was summarily dismissed. I went back to the training area not sure of what had just happened to me. Our company sergeant was a regular army man. When he heard about my experience, he tried very hard to convince me to go to OCS. I couldn't relate to his argument so did not go to OCS. This is one of my youthful mistakes.

I finished my training at Camp Roberts as a PFC, and as a Browning automatic rifleman (BAR). I was never really an expert shot, but I was pretty good. After basic training, I found myself on a train bound for Seattle. When I arrived it was cold, but the barracks was heated with coal. Apparently, I was the only one who knew how to start a fire in a coal stove, so I taught men in several barracks the art of using coal. I was made an acting platoon sergeant in charge of my barracks.

We were in Seattle less than a month when we shipped out. As the Platoon Sergeant, I was told to evacuate the barracks with all of our gear right after breakfast. We then stood outside waiting for further instructions. Finally, an officer came and stood on my left. He commanded those to his left to take one step left and those on his right one step right. Then trucks came to take us to the docks where we shipped out. Those on the left went to the South Pacific, and those to the right to the Aleutian Islands. This was the first time that I had been on a ship, and this one was an old WW I captured German ship with Kaiser Wilhelm's name still in the engine room.

We left Seattle at the end of the day in a convoy of several ships. When we got out to sea, the convoy turned left, but my ship went straight. We had no idea where we were going. The troops quickly became busy with poker and dice games. I was assigned a hammock next to a passageway. I was in bed when there was a very loud BANG, and men were rushing by my bed yelling that we had been torpedoed. We had merely hit rough seas and had encountered a 20- or 30-foot wave. With the rough seas, I was one of a very few who was not seasick. I enjoyed going to the fantail and watching the screws come out of the water.

When we reached land, we were at Kodiak Island. We were given beds in a barracks and assigned to the 201st Infantry, a West Virginia National Guard outfit. I was demoted to Corporal. We now learned that we were originally supposed to go to Kiska as replacements in the Ninth Division, but they had defeated the Japanese before we arrived, therefore we went to Kodiak. We only had one very brief contact with the Japanese on Kodiak Island. Some Zeros came over in fog, and without good radar, they left us alone.

We had nothing to do on Kodiak, so some of the officers located some light tanks and asked for volunteers to operate them. I volunteered as a tank driver. I had operated a track-laying tractor on farms, so driving a tank was easy, but the noise was terrible. The Continental radial aircraft engine that powered the tank was started with a 12-gauge shotgun shell. The shell was placed into a receptacle in the dash and fired. The noise from the explosion was awful inside the metal chamber where I sat.

I was on Kodiak Island for six or seven months before being shipped to Fort George G. Mead, Maryland. I was assigned to a Headquarters Company and to S4 which handles food. There my job was to go to the Central Commissary five days a week in 6X6 trucks to get food for distribution to the mess halls of our battalion. I saw many German prisoners of war at the Commissary doing menial jobs in the area. Which reminds me, there were also thousands of Italian POWs at Fort Mead. Somewhere along the line, I was promoted to Sergeant.

After VE (Victory in Europe) Day I was transferred to Camp Adair, Oregon. This Camp had been reopened sometime before we arrived. We were feeding the troops who were being shipped to the Japanese front. I was at Camp

Adair when the Japanese were defeated. I was then sent back to Fort Mead for discharge.

Following discharge, I married Beatrice Helen Dolan in Laurel, Maryland. We caught a train to Denver, Colorado, because I wanted to go to Veterinary School in Fort Collins, Colorado. When we arrived, there was no space left for us to live there, or for me to attend classes. We caught a Greyhound bus to Cheyenne, Wyoming, where we heard there were jobs. It took most of a month to find a job driving a city bus. I did that for a few months, then got a job in an oil refinery where I worked for six years. A major reason for this was that while I was on Kodiak, I got a middle-ear infection that became chronic, therefore, untreatable. While at the refinery I spent two sessions in a VA hospital in Denver to get treatment for my draining ear, all to no avail. During this time we had four children, three boys, and a girl. The girl Connie died at 3 days of age.

I could see no future at the refinery, so I quit. Soon after that, I learned that I still had time to go to college under the GI Bill. We were living in Coeur d'Alene, Idaho. With three young boys, I enrolled at the University of Idaho. There I earned two degrees; a Bachelor's degree in Agriculture and a Masters in Nutrition. I enjoyed school, so I decided to continue on to a Ph.D. We arrived in Davis, California, in September 1956 to begin work on a degree in Comparative Physiology. Four years later the degree work was completed, and I was given an Assistant Professorship at the University of Alberta, Canada. Three years later I was back at the University of California at Davis. There was a four-year hiatus in the Imperial Valley before returning to the Davis campus, where I remained on the faculty until retirement in 1991.

*Following retirement, I volunteered to videotape the oral histories of retired UC Davis professors. I did this work for 16 years. As my eyesight and hearing began to fail, I decided that it was time to fully retire, done in 2004. My wife and I moved into URC in 2002*

# "Once a Marine, Always a Marine"

## Betty Pearson

I was an officer in the United States Marine Corps Women's Reserve for the last two years of the war – 1943 to 1945. But it was not my first choice.

During my final semester in college, my philosophy professor urged me to enter a national competition an essay I had written about the moral imperative of integrating public schools, and to my surprise and delight, I won a two-year scholarship to Columbia University to do graduate work.

At this point perhaps I should explain to those of you who have never been to Mississippi that the South at that time was a very patriarchal and family-oriented society, and there were strict standards about what a proper "lady" should and should not do. I had a very strong and controlling father, and when I told him I was planning to go to New York to graduate school, he went through the roof. In fact, he was horrified that I would even consider such a thing. We had no family in New York, it was a dangerous city, especially for a young girl alone, and it was in the NORTH for heaven's sake. Had I lost my mind? We had a huge fight, but at 21 I was too young and naïve and still too tied to him and my family to defy him, so I turned down the scholarship. But I was furious at having lost that opportunity, and the week after graduation, in the mood of "I'll show him," I drove to Memphis, 75 miles to the north, and enlisted in the Marine Corps. The Corps was looking for women officers to replace men for combat, and if you had a college degree and could successfully complete boot camp and then Officer Candidate School, you were commissioned a second lieutenant.

When I went home and told my parents what I had done, the "I'll show him" part fizzled out. My father, like most Southern men, was super-patriotic, and he thought it was wonderful. He was very proud of me.

I went to Camp Lejeune in North Carolina for boot camp, which was a shocking change from everything I had ever known. It was challenging, both physically and emotionally. Most high school graduates who had worked in factories or stores, and they were from all over the country. Getting to know them and becoming friends was, I realized later, an important part of my education as an officer.

There was the shock of being awakened at five o'clock every morning by the lights coming on and a loud "Hit the deck!" followed by calisthenics, followed by having just enough time to brush your teeth and then a double-time march to the mess hall for breakfast, then double-time back to clean the barracks for inspection, then on to classes, or close-order drill, or a couple of times a week the obstacle course. We were divided into platoons to learn to march, and after the first couple of weeks, every weekend we had to dress in full uniform, first stand for inspection, then March in review.

Close-order drill and the classes in military etiquette and terminology were conducted by weather-beaten DIs — sergeants, many of them dating back to the peace-time Corps, all of them furious that women had been allowed to become Marines. Their preferred method of instruction was to get right in your face and scream at you at the top of their lungs, and if you couldn't take it, too bad, you washed out. In spite of never having enough time to do everything you had to do, and being constantly chewed out for doing it wrong, or for saying floor instead of deck or wall instead of a bulkhead, or not saluting properly, in spite of never having enough sleep, I have to say that I enjoyed boot camp. Part of the enjoyment was being away from home and on my own, and part was the satisfaction of finding out that I could do everything that was being demanded of me.

After successfully completing boot camp, I and one other woman in my class were promoted to PFC and went directly to Officer Candidate School, still at Camp Lejeune, but in another area. We were immediately aware that OCS was a different world than boot camp. There were no screaming DIs, we were treated as potential officers, but at the same time, the expectations were far greater.

For the first time, I fully realized that I was being trained to be an officer so that I could relieve a man for combat duty. There was a far greater sense of seriousness and purpose, and it was reflected in the number of people washing out. Every few days I would miss someone I had seen the day before. They just seemed to disappear while we were asleep or in class, and I was determined not to have that happen to me.

We studied the history of the Marine Corps, what the Marines had done and were doing in the Pacific, and especially what it meant to be a Marine officer. The basic unit of the Marine Corps is the platoon, and a second lieutenant commands each platoon, and we learned that for a second lieutenant, the highest value is the safety and well-being of the enlisted personnel in the platoon.

By the time we graduated every person in our company was convinced that the Marine Corps was by far the best of the armed forces and that we were privileged to be given the opportunity to become a Marine officer. I received my commission in May 1943, was assigned to Marine Aviation, and spent the rest of the war in southern California, first at El

Toro near Anaheim, and finally at the Naval Air Station on North Island, San Diego.

I was in an Engineer Battalion. We had three huge hangars on the Air Station. An aircraft carrier would dock full of Corsairs and dive bombers that had seen months of service in combat, and our job was to bring them back to A-1 condition, repairing the engine or putting in a new engine, bringing the instruments up-to-date, repairing the bodies, painting them, etc. We had a small group of pilots who had already had a tour of duty in the Pacific and were here as a sort of cushy assignment before they had to go back into combat. Their job was to put engine time on the planes before we put them on a carrier to be returned to the war.

My title was Communications Officer, which covered both mail and official communications from Washington, but most important were all of the service bulletins and specifications on the airplanes which we received, filed and then gave to the appropriate shop when the planes came in. So when a particular airplane came in, the officer in charge of the instrument shop, for example, would be sent the upgrades on all of the instruments, and the officer in charge of the machine shop would be sent the specs on what to do to the body of the plane, etc.

I had 18 or 20 enlisted women working as file clerks, typists, etc., and an old Marine top sergeant as my second-in-command. The officer I had relieved had left some time before my arrival and the sergeant had been running the office, and as far as I could see, doing a good job. He had been with the First Marines on Guadalcanal, and of course had far more experience than I. I knew we had to be friends or my life would be miserable, so I had a heart-to-heart with him. I said that I was sure he was annoyed that women were now Marines, but that he should give us credit for wanting to be one of the best, that I realized he had done a good job running the office and that I would offer him a deal: he could continue to run the day-to-day operation on his own, putting on my desk anything I needed to sign, and getting to me immediately with anything that needed to go to the commanding officer so that I could deliver it right away. I wouldn't look over his shoulder or interfere with how he was running things unless he screwed up, and then it would be his neck. He grinned and said, "It's a deal, Lieutenant" and we got along fine from then on.

Being in aviation, we were a squadron rather than a company, with each lieutenant commanding a section – communications in my case, or the engine shop, or instruments, etc. We had both men and women under our command, with women gradually replacing men in as many positions as possible. For example, when I got there, most of the airplane mechanics were men, with an increasing number of women coming in after having received special training.

Being in San Diego was probably the best assignment it was possible to have in any of the services. The weather is perfect. The Coronado Hotel, that beautiful white pile of wood, was Navy and Marine headquarters on weekends and whenever we were off duty. Tijuana, just across the border in Mexico, was a short drive away, and there were no border restrictions. In Mexico, everything that was rationed or impossible to get in the States was for sale in a thriving black market. And we frequently caught a ride with one of our pilots putting engine time on a plane and flew to San Francisco for a few hours, or just flew out over the ocean or the desert just for the fun of flying.

I think that joining the Marine Corps was the single most important thing I've ever done for myself. I had led a very sheltered life, in a small town where everyone knew me and my family. The Corps gave me a chance to grow up, to separate from my parents, to prove myself on my own terms with no help from family, and to make friends with a wide variety of men and women from all over the country. It was a wonderful and educational experience, and it has enriched my life.

I once told a young Marine officer that I was an ex-Marine. He said, "There is no such thing as an ex-Marine – once a Marine, always a Marine!" I'm very proud to be a Marine.

*After World War II, I married Bill Pearson whom I had known from age five in our native Mississippi. Bill was a fighter pilot in the War. We married in 1947 and spent nearly 50 years on the family plantation. In addition to being an innovator in the cotton industry, we were both active in the Civil Rights movement.*

*We moved to URC from Sumner, Mississippi, in 2008. Our only child Erie is director of the Art Center in Davis. Bill and I have been active in resident affairs including my term as President of the Resident Council followed by a second term as the First Resident Director on the URCAD Board. Unfortunately, we lost Bill in 2017.*

# Landing Signal Officer

## Jim Quick

I was born and raised in Fresno, enrolled at Fresno State in the fall of 1941, and of course, Pearl Harbor in December altered my educational plans. I enlisted in the Navy's V-5 program in October of 1942 to go into flight training. I finally got instructions to go to San Francisco to be inducted.

From there they sent me to a CPT training course in northeastern California near Quincy. A private field there had a contract with the Navy to give V-5 students flight instruction in really small airplanes. An interesting aspect of this training was that since it was winter, the snows had come, and we trained with skis instead of wheels.

Following this training, I went to St. Mary's College in Moraga for pre-flight school - half academic and half tough physical training, and then on to Los Alamitos NAS in Southern California at a brand new airfield built for an operating squadron—big long runways, new buildings, but for some reason they weren't ready to move a squadron in there, so my group did primary training there. Halfway through their training, they moved us to Dallas, TX, to finish primary training. From there, on to intermediate school, and finally I was commissioned with my wings in February of 1943. Then I finished training on single-engine fighter F6F's in Melbourne, Florida.

After that training, fliers were usually assigned to squadrons, but I was selected to do additional flight training to become a Landing Signal Officers (LSO) as well as a pilot, and then assigned to a squadron training in Creed, Virginia, doing "field" carrier landing practice. When the time came for the squadron to go to sea, I would be going with them as their LSO. That's the way the Navy rotated their landing signal officers out at sea.

We soon got orders to go to San Diego, and after some home leave, boarded a "Jeep" carrier used to transport new planes out to the Pacific Theater. I had had little experience at sea and became seasick within an hour. We went to the Hawaiian Islands, did some training there, and then flew from island to island and on to Leyte Gulf in the Philippines where we joined the *USS Independence*.

The head LSO had been on the ship for an extended cruise and was very tired. When we did our first training on the ship, he became confident enough in my performance that after we got out to sea, he said, "I'm going down below deck, it's yours, you know these pilots well enough." He was just worn to a frazzle. So I got to be the head LSO very early on board. This squadron had some very, very, good experienced pilots on their second trip out, along with some new ones. You get to know the individual pilots and their idiosyncrasies—you know what they can do, and which ones you need to treat more carefully.

I had one event when one of the new pilots that had never been at sea before did not respond well to my instructions. This is the first thing pilots have to learn in training is that when the LSO gives an instruction, you have to respond instantaneously; you don't have time to think it over. When you do give the signal to "cut" and land, it is the pilot's prerogative to change his mind if he is confident that he can, and that's what happened to this fellow. He did not respond to the signals I gave him, and he got too low and too slow. It looked as though he was going to crash into the end of the deck so I gave him a wave off, and he was slow in responding to that. He tried to make a turn away from the carrier but was so low that his hook did catch on the arresting wire so he just did a big loop away from the ship and went down into the water with the cable still attached to his hook. So now the ship was dragging the plane backwards through the water. The ship was probably doing 35 knots so it took quite a while to slow down. The emergency people immediately threw him a line with a buoy on it and that person had good aim because it went right across the cockpit, which was filling with water, so the pilot grabbed the line, flipped his safety belt, got out of the plane and was pulled over to the ship and up onto one of the shields over the propellers and up onto the deck unharmed. Finally, they had to take a big fire ax and chop through the 3-inch diameter arresting cable to let the plane go.

Another event was when one of the pilots made a good approach and landing, but the hook snapped off when it grabbed the wire, and the plane just rolled on up the deck. There was a safety barrier about four feet off the deck, and the plane rolled into that, flipped over and was stopped. The problem was that he had an external belly fuel tank with a lot of gas in it. His maneuver ripped that open, and immediately there were flames all over. I looked around the plastic windbreak that I was working in front of and suddenly saw a fog of gas vapor that burst into a ball of flame. They quickly doused the fire, and the pilot was not hurt.

We were on station about three months and did lose several planes in combat. It went fairly routinely until one morning we had a strike out: and we suddenly got the orders to have all the planes return to the ship, and they announced that the war was over. So I was not at sea for a long period and was glad that it was over.

*My wife Betty and I both grew up in the Fresno area. We married after the interruption of my college days by my service in the Navy. After completing my education at Fresno State I began my career as a chemist for the Agriculture Extension Service. I transferred to the main office in Berkeley and then to Davis in1959, retiring in 1986.*

*Betty and I moved to a cottage at URC in 2009 where we were able to slow down from active volunteer work in Fresno, Walnut Creek, and Davis. We had three children, four grandchildren, and two great-granddaughters. One daughter lives in Sacramento and a son lives in Washington state.*

# Ego Trip with the Army Air Force

## Jack Suder

I grew up in Somerset, Pennsylvania, and was 16 when I heard of the attack on Pearl Harbor. Somerset was a small rural community of approximately 6,000 residents, and little seemed to change with the announcement. I was able to pursue my strong interest in aviation by taking flying lessons in a Model J-3 Piper Cub - and my even stronger interest in schoolmate Hazel Baker, who would be the love of my life for 75 years. Upon graduation in 1943, I received "two life-altering documents:" my high school diploma and my draft notice.

When I reported to the Induction Center, I thought I would end up in the infantry since I was about 5'8" tall and weighed about 120 pounds, the processing personnel must have thought I was "too skinny to carry a rifle and a field pack." So they assigned me to the Army Air Force as an aviation cadet. The fact that I already had some 5-6 hours of dual flight training likely aided in that decision.

I was sent for basic training to Greensboro, NC, and then to pre-flight training at Maxwell Field in Montgomery, Alabama. After pre-flight training, I was sent to Souther Field in Americus, Georgia, for flight training on the Northrup PT-17. Although the normal washout rate of student pilots was over 30%, I successfully made it through and was then sent to Gunter Field (Montgomery, Alabama) for basic flight training in the Boeing BT-13, better known amongst its pilots as the Vultee Vibrator.

Advanced flight training was at Craig Field, Selma, Alabama, in the North American AT-6 and then the Famous Curtis P-40. In December 1944, I completed my flight training and received my fighter pilot's wings and my commission as a Second Lieutenant.

After a ten-day leave, I returned to base fully expecting to receive orders to report to a fighter squadron in Europe, but to my surprise, the top 30% of my graduating class was ordered to report to Amarillo, Texas, to begin training to become B-29 flight engineers. The following months were devoted to an intensive training course on the various systems that made the B-29 work.

I was then sent to a large base at Alamogordo, New Mexico, where I was assigned to an aircrew and subjected to additional intensive in-flight training. The crew was declared ready for combat and assigned a new B-29 and placed on orders to fly to the South Pacific. But, the next day the pilot (airplane commander) was hospitalized with appendicitis. Since I was now a member of a trained aircrew, orders were put on hold for 30 days while the pilot recovered from an appendectomy.

After a month, orders to go to the South Pacific were again activated, but a week later the atom bombs were dropped on Hiroshima and Nagasaki. The Japanese surrendered, and the war was over. All orders for deployment were canceled.

I spent the last half of 1945 waiting to be released from active duty and taking several mail-order courses with the Armed Forces Institute that I hoped would be accepted for credit towards graduation once I was in college. In December

1945 I was sent to Mitchell Field for separation and finished processing in time to be home for the Christmas holidays.

I think of my time in the AAF as the best ego trip an 18-20-year-old kid could have and I credit learning self-sufficiency from my military life.

Hazel had promised to write a letter every day while I was away, and that was a promise that she kept. I entered Franklin Marshall College in Lancaster, Pennsylvania, where I majored in chemistry and graduated in 1948. Hazel had been attending Drexel Institute of Technology majoring in Biochemistry. She finished second in her class and graduated with honors.

Hazel and I were married in 1948, after Hazel graduated and during my last semester. We both were accepted for graduate study at Penn State. In 1954 we both received master's degrees, and in 1956, we both were awarded Ph.D.'s.

After graduation, I was hired by the Dupont Company as a research chemist and Hazel was hired by the University of Delaware to teach Bio-chemistry. After a year of teaching, Hazel quit working to become a stay-at-home mom and spent the next 15 years raising three sons.

*In 1959 the family moved to California where I was hired by Aerojet as manager of liquid propellant chemistry lab. Hazel returned to teaching as a professor of Nutrition at Sacramento State University in 1972. In 1972 I was hired by the California Air Resources Board as manager of the atmospheric chemistry and research department. Both Hazel and I retired in 1987. We moved to URC in 2002. I lost my beloved Hazel in 2015.*

# From Internment Camp to US Army Headquarters

## George Suzuki

Before 1942, my world was centered in Sacramento's Japantown. I was born in Acampo, California, near Stockton, and my family moved to Sacramento where I attended Lincoln Elementary, Sacramento High and Sacramento Junior College. I was an active Boy Scout and explored the Sierra Nevada mountains on fishing expeditions with my father.

In 1942, I was enrolled at Sacramento Jr. College, my brother Masamichi (Mac) was in his second year at UC San Francisco Medical School, and my younger sister Mariko was in high school. (My brother Minoru, adopted by an uncle, was in Japan.) As a result of President Roosevelt's Executive Order 9066, my family and I were among the 110,000 Japanese-Americans removed from the Western Defense Zone and detained, first at Walerga Assembly Center and then at Tule Lake Relocation Center, both in California. I soon discovered that the Quaker-led National Japanese American Student Relocation Council (NJASRC) would help students transfer to colleges outside the exclusion area, and at the suggestion of one my professors I applied to the University of Wisconsin, Madison, Wisconsin. I was accepted, but the Army would not let me leave Tule Lake, saying that there was classified research ongoing in Madison.

Next, I applied to Ohio University, Athens, Ohio. Again, the university accepted me, but the Army would not let me leave Tule Lake because of a race riot in Athens. (The riot involved African-Americans not Japanese-Americans.) I successfully enrolled at the University of Denver, only to discover that the statistics professor had joined the military, at which point I changed my major to Business Administration. On graduation, I did graduate studies in statistics at the University of Minnesota. (Through the NJASRC, over 5,500 Nisei left the camps to attend college.)

I was drafted into the army in mid-1945, took my basic training at Camp Robinson, Arkansas, and after basic, I was sent to Fort Snelling, Minnesota, to await the start of the language class for the military intelligence service.

While I was waiting, I applied to a new army technical division in Washington, D. C. I was accepted and assigned to the Research and Development section of the General Staff. Recalling the Army's objection to my attendance at the University of Wisconsin in 1942 on the grounds of the ongoing classified research at the University, I found it ironic that this new assignment was in an office requiring very high-security clearance. I spent the rest of my army career in Washington, D. C.

One week before the start of the school term in the fall of 1947, a Dean at the University of Minnesota was without a statistics instructor. He offered the position to me while I was still in the Army. At that time, there was a critical shortage of University faculty, and the Army readily released qualified individuals. My discharge was expedited; within 3 days, I was discharged; within a week, I was teaching statistics at the University.

*After my discharge, I returned to the University of Minnesota where I continued my graduate studies and taught statistics. After receiving my Ph.D. I worked for the Air Force, the Navy and the National Bureau of Standards doing consulting work in the area of Operational Research. While in Washington, D.C. my wife June received her Masters of Library Science from Catholic University. She worked in a variety of libraries (government, college, medical and public.)*

*After retirement, we moved to Incline Village on Lake Tahoe where we lived for twenty years. We both loved nature and the outdoors and enjoyed hiking, cross country skiing and the company of new-found friends. We moved to Reno as a transition to retirement. While there we visited a friend at Rogue Valley Manor and learned about URC.*

# War Worker to Aviation Cadet to Marine

## Frank Vasek

I was born in 1927 and was among the younger World War II veterans. Growing up in Depression-era Maple Heights, Ohio, I was expected to work to help my family. I had a regular newspaper route delivering the afternoon *Cleveland Press* until mid-1942 and picked up additional income selling magazines door-to-door.

I delivered mail at Christmas from 1941 to 1945 and worked after school in the winter and spring of 1943-44 as a swing mail carrier and post office janitor, which included mopping out the lobby and carrying out the ashes from the furnace.

My early memories are colored by lows and highs of the war effort. I remember an air of deep despair after the attack on Pearl Harbor, when America was suddenly fully engaged. (While the Japanese attack swept away most opposition to entering the war, I had the sense that the release of the movie *Sergeant York* before Pearl Harbor did a lot to pull Americans out of isolationism and prepare the nation for war.) The emotional low of Pearl Harbor was offset five months later by Jimmy Doolittle's bombing raid on Tokyo, giving Americans the sense that their forces could effectively strike the Japanese homeland. Further encouragement came from the successful landings in North Africa that opened an additional front against the Axis powers.

I was aware of my role in delivering good and bad news as I made my rounds with newspapers and mail. I remember carrying the blue-tinted, postage-free V-mail letters to families of servicemen; it gave me satisfaction to know the family was going to get news from their loved one. There were times I'd deliver 10-20 letters to a family at once because of delays in getting mail out of the war zones and back to the US.

In the summer of 1942, I found work in a machine shop that made chemical mortar shells—one of many high school students filling the labor gap. Another summer I worked at a dog food plant that had been adapted to packing canned pork for Lend-Lease shipment to Russia. I stacked the filled cans into retorts to be cooked and sterilized in steam boilers. After that, sealed cans were boxed (62 pounds per box) and loaded onto trucks for shipment to the rail yard (3 trucks per boxcar).

Other jobs I did included packing pipe fittings and part-time landscaping. To support the war effort, I canvassed for scrap metal all over Southeast Cleveland and its suburbs, took fat to the butcher shop, and worked on paper drives.

I wanted to join the Army Air Corps as a fighter pilot, so I enlisted in the Air Corps Reserves in June of 1944. The Air Corps soon had mastery of the air in Europe and began reducing their recruiting program. As a consequence, I was offered a choice between a transfer elsewhere in the Army or a redeployment discharge. It looked to me like the war in Europe was nearly over, but the Japanese war was not. I therefore elected the redeployment discharge, which was effective May 11, 1945, and I enlisted immediately in the

Marine Corps. By May 24 I was on a train bound for Marine Corps boot camp at Parris Island, S.C. I finished basic training and was home on boot leave when the Pacific war ended on VJ Day. I remember exuberant celebrations.

Instead of being sent to Japan, I was sent to the Marine Corps Radio Operator School in the Philadelphia Navy Yard. The Marine Corps was rapidly being demobilized in 1946, but the State Department saw troublesome potential events in the Caribbean area. Consequently, an Expeditionary Unit (called the First Special Marine Brigade) was pulled together from new recruits, instructors in Marine schools, and some regulars whose enlistments had not yet run out, especially from the Second Marine Division. I was assigned to the Headquarters Company, which was transported on the AKA 97, the *USS Merrick*. One infantry battalion was transported on the APA 219, and the Second Infantry Battalion was transported on six US Navy destroyers. This flotilla sailed to Puerto Rico for amphibious landing training, and then just happened to be cruising three miles off the Haitian coast when Haiti was having an election. However, the Haitian Army allowed the election to proceed, and hence trouble did not develop. I was discharged on August 22, 1946.

I started college right away at Kent State University and then later transferred to Ohio University. During that first year, the Marine Corps sent recruiting officers to campus to enroll ex-Marines in a program to train Reserve Platoon Leaders. I joined up again and spent the summers of 1946 and 1947 training at the Marine Corps Base at Quantico, VA. I graduated from Ohio U. in 1950, and was just preparing to start graduate work at UCLA when the Korean War broke out. I fully expected to be called up and sent to Korea very soon. However, during the physical exam, I was found to have high blood pressure; I was rejected by the Marine Corps and subsequently discharged.

Looking back, I feel I happened to benefit from avoiding two tragic events. One is that the atomic bomb was dropped just as I was finishing boot camp. That ended the war and made the forceful and costly invasion of Japan unnecessary. The second event was the high blood pressure, which precluded the expected and dangerous experience of leading an infantry platoon in combat.

*After leaving the Marine Corps I earned a PhD in Botany. While at UCLA I met my wife Maxine McClellen. My first faculty position was at the newly-formed University of California at Riverside, and retired 34 years later as a Professor of Botany.*

*Upon retirement we travelled extensively followed by 10 years on an avocado grove near Escondido. We moved to Davis to be near a daughter living there for 13 years before moving to URC in 2013.*

# Travel with the US Army

## Wilbur Ray Vincent

I was raised on a farm in the central part of the lower peninsula of Michigan along with four brothers. My parents encouraged my interest in science, and while I was in high school, my father took me to Detroit to take an examination for an amateur radio license. I passed the examination. This was shortly followed by another trip to take the test for a commercial radio license.  (As a very young high-school student, my goal was to be a Marine radio operator and see the world.) I passed this two-day examination. These two events had an immense impact on later life.

At the start of World War II, I was a sophomore engineering student at Michigan State College, working in Radio Station WKAR to cover expenses. Most of the men took ROTC, and many, including me, signed up for the reserves. This allowed us to complete the winter and spring quarters before being called for active duty.

After basic training at Jefferson Barracks, MO, I was sent to Grinnell College in Iowa for processing, and then on to North Carolina State College in Raleigh, NC, under the Army Specialized Training program (ASTP). After nine months at

North Carolina State, I received orders to Fort Monmouth, NJ, for three months of intensive training on specialized radio equipment. On completion of that program, I became a part of a small unit that was sent to the Lebanon State Park in NJ, a holding location isolated from other military units and from the general population. We were not allowed to leave the location.

At this location, we met our Master Sergeant, a former labor-union organizer and enforcer from the Brooklyn docks. He was a grizzled and crusty man, much older than any of us and he had a nasty reputation based on labor-union organization work among Brooklyn dockyards. It was clear that he was assigned to teach us young and raw college kids a bit of discipline. At the state park, our duties were minimal but included fighting a forest fire. On the way to it, the military truck turned a corner too sharply, fell on its side, and spilled us raw recruits riding in its rack into a ditch. That ended the fire-fighting task. Other than broken eyeglasses and a few bruises, I survived.

After a short period, we received orders to travel to an unknown destination by train. We were assigned to a coach car, and it headed west. That crafty, old, and grizzly Master Sergeant, however, traveled by air. As a lowly and inexperienced Private First Class (PFC), completely ignorant of the duties required to guide sixteen erratic and high-spirited young men to some unknown destination; I was put in charge of the unit.

It soon became obvious that the train was headed in a Westerly direction. Since train tracks follow well-defined paths, it became clear that it was headed through the mid-western home towns of a couple of my fellow soldiers. I allowed them to call their parents, who then showed up at the train stop in their home town. The parents then drove their soldier sons to the next stop thirty or forty miles further along the track, allowing them to have brief family reunions. Fortunately, the train stopped at each town, and they all reappeared. That train finally arrived at Camp Stoneman (it no longer exists) near Pittsburg, CA. As a lowly PFC who had no idea about proper military procedures, I provided passes for the fellows to spend a few hours in the local towns since we all sensed that our last hours in the USA were fast approaching.

After three days, we were herded onto a ferry boat which headed for San Francisco. It docked at a Fisherman's Wharf pier, where we met up with our crusty Master Sergeant. He directed us across the pier and onto the USS Sea Ray, a new Liberty Ship. That walk across the pier was the total extent of my first visit to the fabled city of San Francisco. We had no knowledge about the ship's next port, but all hoped for Hawaii. We were assigned bunks in a hold and proceeded to get acquainted with our new home.

First on my agenda, along with several fellow soldiers, was a trip to the latrine. There we found the crusty old Master Sergeant hunched over the long urinal trough, up-chucking his recent meal. He became seasick while the ship was still tied to the dock, and he never recovered. The crowning blow was when he went to urinate and his false teeth fell into the urinal. I watched him recover and shake the urine off his dripping teeth while others were lined up using the urinal. At that moment our crusty old Master Sergeant completely lost his influence and control over us. He instantly became an ordinary human being. He was seasick for the entire voyage from San Francisco to our destination, Milne Bay, at the southern tip of New Guinea. We became a free-spirited group of young college kids out to explore the world without professional guidance from our Master Sergeant. On arrival at Milne Bay, our Master Sergeant was transferred to a Hospital ship to return to the USA.

While spending 10 months at an isolated location near Milne Bay, I developed a serious case of jungle rot and was scheduled for medical evacuation home as a useless soldier. But, General MacArthur had other plans—such as invading the Philippines. Every spare body in the Pacific region that could walk was assigned to that task. My small unit was ordered to immediately board a rusty old tramp ship for the trip north. On the way up the gangplank, dressed only in GI under-shorts because of the jungle rot and with a body purple from ineffective potassium-permanganate treatments, I heard the ship's loader holler "Those with Thompson and Grease machine guns live on deck. Those with carbines go below." My friend in the line ahead of me had a Grease gun, but wanted to go below. With my sad case of jungle rot and a carbine, I wanted the deck. We swapped guns on the way up the gangplank and both met our goals.

That old tub immediately left Milne Bay, and it joined a large convoy heading north. Most of the deck space was occupied by loaded trucks, and the experienced GIs claimed sleeping space on top of their loads and under the weather protection provided by the truck's canvas covering. I put a cargo net on top of a mixture of oxygen and acetylene bottles stacked at the deck's edge and pitched my pup tent. It was a poor living place in case of trouble, but it was comfortable and a few feet above the wet deck.

Next, it was time to explore the features and conveniences available on that fine old tub. First, we found the cooks setting up a field kitchen on an open portion of the deck. Then it was time to find a way to cope with nature. There was no room for a GI latrine on the old tub, but that problem was solved by running some heavy timbers out beyond the deck and building a makeshift latrine well outside the safety of the steel deck. It was a new experience to sit with ones' rear-end exposed to the open sea and salt spray. There was no EPA or OSHA to prohibit the operation of such a simple and effective facility.

After traveling a few nautical miles from the dock we realized this might be a difficult trip when that rusty old tub backed onto a reef and bent its propeller shaft. That caused the deck to go up and down with each rotation of the propeller shaft. That old tub was the slowest ship in the convoy. Then we entered a tropical storm, and a navy destroyer came alongside. With the aid of a bull horn, its Captain announced in very plain, easy-to-understand, navy language, that we would be abandoned if the ship could not make 8 knots. Our Captain ordered more speed since he wanted the protection of the U.S. Navy, but the shaking and vibration of the entire ship was too much. That old tub was shaking apart. We were abandoned to proceed northward, all alone, at a leisurely 3 to 4 knots, exposed to aircraft and submarine attack without U.S. Navy protection.

Shortly after leaving Milne Bay it became evident why those with Thompson and Grease guns were ordered to live on the deck. The ship's Captain was deathly afraid of air and submarine attack. His ship had no armor, and I instantly became an antiaircraft gunner—with a lowly and ineffective Grease gun. One could take a Grease gun apart and throw the pieces at an airplane with more effect than shooting at one. Next, the ship's Captain asked if anyone could copy Morse code. I was a good Morse-code operator and in younger days had dreamed of traveling the world as a ship's radioman. The opportunity arrived since that rusty old ship had a radio room, but it had only one radio operator. I instantly became his alternate while we proceeded slowly north, all alone, in the tropical seas at 4 knots maximum speed.

Because the trip north took 37 days at our slow pace, we missed the initial Philippine invasion of the island of Leyte and were redirected to be off-loaded at the Lingayen Gulf north of Manila, a beautiful place. As we entered the gulf, I climbed the mast and crawled out on a yardarm to get a better view of the sights. That aroused the wrath of the ship's Captain who opened his bridge window, shook his fist at me and hollered some choice words which were lost to the distance and wind. While he was shaking his fist and hollering, a Japanese cannon in a cave on a nearby hill lobbed a shell at his rusty old ship. That shell crossed the ship halfway between the Captain and me and splashed harmlessly into the water. Seeing that shell pass about 40-feet away clearly altered the Captain's mental state. He slammed his bridge window shut and decided other duties were more pressing than dealing with an idiot out on the yardarm—like saving his rusty old tub. He left me alone to view the scenery as he proceeded further into the gulf to anchor his ship in the middle of this idyllic place.

Our little unit arrived at the alternate location in the Philippines, safe and sound, after a leisurely cruise in the tropical waters of the western Pacific Ocean. Thirty-seven days of on-deck living completely cured the jungle rot, and it has never returned.

Since we were late in arriving at the Philippines, the time had overcome the need for our little unit, and we were placed in a variety of isolated holding locations near Manila with little to do except become acquainted with the Philippines. Shortly, we were gathered together and trucked to Clark AFB where seven airplanes were lined up to take us and our equipment to the next unknown destination. The plane landed at what is now the Naha International Airport on Okinawa, but it was a bare runway at that time. We were trucked through the capital, Naha, and on to Northern Okinawa. I still remember that nothing was standing in Naha higher than 2-feet-above ground.

The truck delivered us to a new radio-intercept site where my position was as an operator and maintenance guy of radio equipment installed in a tent. Among other things that tent contained the best radio receiver available and a teletype machine with a direct radio link to Manila where General MacArthur had his headquarters. I spent hours and hours with that receiver listening to Japanese and other radio signals. I had become proficient in the International Morse Code as a radio amateur in high school days and taught myself Japanese Morse code while in the Pacific. Copying clear-text and coded messages provided an odd form of entertainment, and it helped pass the time of day while in that tent.

For several nights Japanese Betty bombers passed over us. We quickly learned their distinct sound, which was much different from our P-47 and P-38 airplanes. The nightly Betty bomber visits abruptly ended when the P-61 Black Widow night fighters began patrolling the skies North of Okinawa.

We all knew that the release of the two atomic bombs meant that the end of the war was imminent, but how imminent was a popular question. None of us relished the thought of participating in an invasion of Japan.

Shortly after the second bomb was dropped, I copied a Morse code message from the military radio-transmitting station in Tokyo that repeated over and over "CQ MACARTHUR DE JAPAN" (Which meant calling MacArthur from Japan,) followed by a notice of total surrender. I typed it all into the teletype machine as it was being received so it could be transmitted directly to Manila on the radio link I controlled for evaluation by General MacArthur's staff—thinking that it just might be important.

Wow, the reply was unexpected and something like this: "we cannot confirm your reception of this signal and quit sending bogus information" followed by a threat of severe disciplinary action. But, I kept resending that message as it was received for two more days, since there was little anyone in distant Manila could do to a lowly corporal in a tent in the boondocks of northern Okinawa. Finally, on the third day of this process, Manila confirmed the reception of the radio signal at their location, and the threat of disciplinary action vanished into thin air.

A short while later, Japanese representatives flew from Japan to the nearby island, Ie Shima, to arrange surrender terms. I was able to monitor the radio transmissions from the primary plane, a Betty bomber familiar to all of us, as it traveled from Japan to Okinawa, and I watched the plane approach and land at Ie Shima. While others with two-way radios handled the primary communications task, I was listening to the messages flowing back and forth in cleartext. I felt it was a part of history and felt relieved because none of us would be needed to participate in the invasion of Japan.

A few weeks later grateful local officers promoted me to return home as a Technical Sergeant. At the end of the war, my little unit was put into a small and isolated holding camp while waiting for transportation home. While in the holding camp, a major typhoon hit Okinawa. Wind-speed meters peaked at 160 mph. There was devastation everywhere. Early in the storm I found an old Japanese cave on the side of a nearby hill, crawled in, and watched big timbers and trash blow past the entrance. The cave was high and dry, a perfect place to sit out the storm.

Finally, space became available for our little unit on a Liberty Ship. We had accumulated a lot of travel points from duty in New Guinea, the Philippines and Okinawa, so we managed to return home to the USA fairly early. Our little unit arrived back in San Francisco and received a nice welcome home from the water jets of fireboats, the horns of sailboats and other blasts from ships in the bay, followed by another train trip across the country to my separation place at Fort Sheridan IL.

That ended my military career. I returned home and went back to Michigan State College, now Michigan State University, and returned to work at the radio station, again to help cover costs, which now included occasional trips home to visit a former coed who had graduated during the war and was now a school teacher in my home town of Midland, MI. We were married while in graduate school, and we had a wonderful life together for 44 years before cancer ended that happy time in life.

Later in life, I made several trips to Okinawa, and I tried to locate the WWII site. The place had changed so much during the post-war times that the site's location could not be found, only the general area. Many other places were identified, but not the one of special interest to me. Naha is now a contemporary city with massive traffic problems, and the island of Okinawa is now a modern and densely-populated place. Okinawa now has beautiful tourist hotels along shorelines that once were deadly places.

On one of several trips to Okinawa, I took a ferry to Ie Shima, the nearby island where the war correspondent Ernie Pyle was killed. I could see that island from my tent during WW II, and I was there when Ernie met his end from a sniper's bullet. All WW II GIs read and valued Ernie's accounts of the war in Stars and Stripes.

I spent some memory time at the Ernie Pyle Memorial on Ie Shima, which is nicely maintained by a small contingent of U.S. Marines located on the island. Tobacco-chewing Corporal Parsley of the US Marines provided me with a VIP tour of the small island with his Marine Corps van. I will never forget Corporal Parsley and his nasty habit of chewing tobacco, frequently spitting tobacco juice out of the window of his van, but I will forever be grateful to him for taking me to the Ernie Pyle Memorial.

*After my discharge from the Army, I returned to Michigan State University where I earned a BS and MS in Electrical Engineering. Upon graduation, I married Dorothy L. Underwood and was employed by Bell Aircraft in Niagara Falls, New York, for eight years working on early supersonic missiles and aircraft. I then worked for Stanford Research Institute in Palo Alto, California, for 20 years. After an interlude in small business and consulting, I was asked to join the staff at the Naval Postgraduate School in Monterey, California, as an associate professor over the next 20 years. While at the NPGS I lost my wife to cancer and remarried Aildene L. Adams of Palo Alto and moved to URC in 2000. Aildene*

*died of cancer in 2008. In August of 2011, I married Georgia L. Paulo.*

*I retired from the Naval Postgraduate School in 2008. I continued to work as a consultant, which provided many opportunities to travel widely and participate in scientific and technical work in 60 overseas locations. I am the author of many technical studies.*

# Yeoman Third Class Yates

## Wesley E. Yates

I volunteered for duty in the US Navy on 12 April 1945 at the age of seventeen. My first assignment was to the Naval Training Center in Great Lakes, IL, for Boot Camp training. On completion of Boot Camp, I was traveling to San Francisco for reassignment when the atomic bombs were dropped on Japan on August 6th and 9th. This was an exhilarating experience to find out I would not have to enter into an active combat area. I was scheduled to participate in an invading Sea Bee (CB) Group.

Subsequently, I was assigned to the *U.S.S. Hercules* AK 41. This ship carried large ammunition supplies for combat operations during the war. Our mission was to carry large ammunition from the South Pacific back to the Brooklyn, NY, Navy Yard. Thus, we sailed without cargo from San Francisco to Manus Island in the Admiralty Islands, located just north of New Guinea on the Eastern edge of the Pacific Ocean (about 2-degrees South of the equator). Our route back was near the equator, directly to the Panama Canal. This was a pleasant trip in very calm waters.

I enjoyed working in the ship's main office, updating personnel records, distributing announcements, etc. We had a few nights shore leave in Panama, then on to the Brooklyn Navy Yard to discharge our cargo. Our ship was then sent to the Norfolk Navy Yard for decommissioning. By the middle of 1946, there was no more need for servicemen, and I typed discharge orders for fellow crew members, including my orders for honorable discharge on 11 July 1946 as a Yeoman Third Class.

I then took advantage of the GI bill to continue my education by enrolling in Morningside College in Sioux City, Iowa, in the fall of 1946.

*On my return to Iowa, I decided to use my G.I. Bill benefits and continue my education. I entered Morningside College in Sioux City, planning to major in agricultural engineering. After one year I transferred to Iowa State College. With Iowa State on the quarter system, I was able to attend summer sessions and complete the four-year program in three years graduating with honors in August 1949 with a BA in Agricultural Engineering. I was encouraged by my mentor at Iowa State to continue my education at the graduate level and recommended me to the Chairman of the Agricultural Engineering Department at the University of California (UCD) at Davis.*

*In September of 1949, I was accepted in the Master of Science Program and had accepted an offer of a Research Assistantship receiving my MS degree in June of 1951 and was offered and accepted a faculty position in July 1951.*

*The work at UCD was not only interesting and rewarding but was indirectly responsible for another important part of my life. Through the wife of a UCD professor, I met Joy Williams. We were married July 11, 1952, and grew our family of two daughters. My work in research and development of aerial spraying techniques would take me worldwide during my 39 year career with UCD. I retired from UCD in July, 1998 and moved to URC in 2000.*

# Back At Home

# Feeders

## A Poem by Lena Cantrell McNicholas

Farm Boys who harvested trees, stoked furnaces,

crawled into dark holes for lumps of coal.

Deer slayers with silent tread, keen eyes and

Deadly bead as they crouched in mountain blinds.

When called they hung aluminum tags

around their high shaved necks and became

hunters of men, returned to hilltop graves

and fed the soil.

*Lena Cantrell McNicholas was born in a small mountain town in Virginia. I consider life an adventure and this trait took me to many places around the world before coming to URC in Davis to be near my sons: Joseph – Sacramento; Michael – Dallas; and Bruce – Seattle.*

*I graduated from Radford College, women's division of Virginia*

*Tech with a BA in social studies followed by bicycling and motoring through Europe with two college friends.*

*After teaching in Virginia, Kentucky and Maryland I accepted a teaching position in Venezuela where I met Pennsylvania geologist George McNicholas, an employee of Gulf Oil. That job took us to Nigeria, now a family of five. Returning to Virginia and then Texas, George accepted a transfer to Walnut Creek after Chevron acquired Gulf Oil where George died in 1987. After his death, I returned to Virginia where I was a caregiver to my mother and later to her younger brother.*

*I arrived at URC in 2011 where I became a member of Performing Arts, play reading, worked on the Bazaar and am a "floating member" of Hospitality. I shared my work with reading on National Poetry Month April 2112, a second reading with portions of her second book in progress.*

*Writing and work became my therapy for many years and it culminated in the publishing of a book entitled Patchwork Pieces of Appalachia, a memoir in poetry, essays, vignettes, and music.*

# There at the Beginning, There at the End
## Dan Cheatham

I was born in June 1936 in the town of Lihue on the island of Kauai in the Territory of Hawaii. My father was the electrical engineer for the sugar plantation in Lihue. He also helped bring electricity to the whole island of Kauai.

My grandparents lived in the territory of Hawaii from 1900. It was still the Kingdom of Hawaii at that time. My grandfather was in Honolulu when the United States Army aboard a naval ship …if it wasn't the Army it would have been Marines… took over the Royal Palace.

In those years the children of the missionaries in the Kingdom reached an age when they became professionals and were starting their own careers. They felt that the Kingdom of Hawaii needed to be part of the United States.

As stated above, there were some troops that marched to the Palace and took over the Kingdom and made it a territory of the United States. Later, my grandparents moved from Honolulu to the island of Kauai. My grandfather became the keeper of the plantation store at one of the sugar plantations. They had children among whom was my father who went to the Mainland long enough to get some engineering education. He had some very interesting adventures hitchhiking around the continental United States on his return to Kauai.

My mother was Russian born and raised in the town of Harbin in Manchuria, China. She got a nursing degree in the city of San Francisco and shortly after graduating she was an accompanying nurse for someone who needed a helper to return with her on a ship to Hawaii. That is how my mother ended up in the town of Lihue where my sister and I were born.

In my youth, each of the islands had its own radio station. Likely because of available technology, one radio station could not be listened to on another island. On our island the station was KTOH.

The population of the Islands was very mixed with Hawaiians, Americans, Chinese, Japanese, and Filipinos. It was the Americans who were in charge. The sugar mills and other plantations were owned by Americans and the schools were taught in English. There were children of the other groups who were not in school. Our school was mostly Americans, referred to as "Haoles."

On Sunday mornings, during breakfast, everyone listened to the radio news. The radio station in Honolulu acted as the master control station. So, on your island you could hear what was happening on the other islands. Each island would chime in with an announcement of what was happening there during the previous week. There were social announcements about who was visiting from the States, extension of the local road system, and other local items of general interest. This weekly radio program served as a nonexistent all-island newspaper. Honolulu had a newspaper, with fewer weekly newspapers on the smaller islands. The Honolulu newspaper could take days, or a week, before reaching the outer islands via boat.

With everyone listening to hear about friends and activities on the other islands, on Sunday, December 7, 1941, there was an announcement that the program was being interrupted to report an attack on Pearl Harbor by the Japanese. The broadcast was at breakfast time. I was only five years old so it didn't mean much to me, but my parents were very concerned. I began to understand that something special was happening. The broadcast continued to report on further developments. The voice was Webley Edwards, if I recall, on station KGMB in Honolulu. Years later, he was the voice on the radio program "Hawaii Calls" which was a tourist-oriented weekly program on the Mainland.

On Kauai, a few weeks after the attack on Pearl Harbor, we had a Japanese submarine shoot its cannon at the harbor in Lihue and set fire to some cane fields. There was a quick assembly of men to take care of these fires. I don't remember, but this attack was likely a couple of weeks after December 7th. It lasted less than an hour. It was the only Japanese involvement the Island of Kauai had during the War.

At the time there was no US military on the island. A small number of military did arrive later. Up to that time the only aircraft with access to the island were American DC-3's. There was an airstrip for them and some P-40 fighters were then based there.

Our house, near the harbor, was right next to a water tower which provided water for the small steam trains that served the cane fields and connected them to the sugar mill. After the fighters chased each other on practice and headed back to their airfield, they would "attack" the water tower. When they did, all conversation in the house would have to stop because of the noise.

Shortly after the Pearl Harbor attack, students in my grammar school were issued gas masks. We would hang them on hooks on the wall outside each classroom. Trenches were dug in the ground near each building in case of another Japanese attack. During air raid drills we would get into the trenches.

For the first several months after the initial attack, no one knew whether the Japanese would attack again. There was great activity in Honolulu with stretching barbed wire along the beaches and digging trenches for defense against any invasion.

Living in Hawaii, I was unaware what was happening to the Japanese on the Mainland which led to their interment in camps in the California desert and elsewhere. (One of these camps is now part of the National Park Service.)

Internment did not happen in Hawaii because there was such a huge Japanese population. Interning the Japanese population in Hawaii would have brought the economy to a stop because they were such a huge part of the economy.

At the time, the Territory of Hawaii was being administered by the U.S. Department of Interior, Office of Territories. The civilian governor was discharged and Washington sent an Army General to become the Governor. The General, when he arrived, saw Japanese wearing Army uniforms serving in active duty. Quite understandably, when the Governor saw the need for military defense, he put the ROTC students at the University on active duty. This General observed these Japanese college students wearing American Army uniforms and he said "No Way." They were removed from the Army. He had absolutely no understanding of the multi-racial life in the Territory of Hawaii. He also saw Japanese civilians functioning normally in everyday life which he found shocking. Island residents started making noise in Washington about the General and he was transferred out.

There was a lot of activity relative to these Japanese students, all of them US Citizens by birth in Hawaii, not being allowed to serve in the military. In the end, Washington agreed to create what was to become known as the 442nd Regimental Combat Team. (There is a Hollywood movie about this unit.) As a result, even many Japanese interned in camps on the Mainland were also allowed to join up with the Japanese from the Territory of Hawaii. As I understand it, the 442nd RCT remains the most highly decorated unit in the American military because of its activity in Europe. There is a monument near Waikiki Beach which honors these Japanese-Americans who served in the US military.

The lifestyle in Hawaii was quite different from the Mainland. All the children in the outer islands went barefoot. I walked to school in bare feet. We walked that way on the streets as well as playing out in the cane fields. Visitors to our household would sit on the porch smoking cigarettes. When they finished they would flick them out on the lawn. I would go out on the lawn and put out the cigarette with my bare feet to indicate how toughened our feet became.

When the time came to go up to the Mainland, my mother and I left Honolulu when I was seven years old. We traveled, with others, on an empty troopship which was returning to the Mainland. Before we got on the ship my mother took me to a store in Honolulu to buy me my first pair of shoes, in what we would call a department store today, in Honolulu. My mother and I got on the ship, my parents were divorced at this point, and we sailed to San Francisco. My sister had left for the Mainland earlier with my grandparents.

The boat docked in San Francisco on, for me, a very eventful afternoon. As we approached the harbor, people went to the front of the ship to see what they called the "Golden Gate," with the setting sun behind us. When the ship docked in San Francisco I was still going barefoot. For quite understandable reasons my mother insisted that I put my shoes on before we got off the ship to catch a taxi cab that would take us to stay with her brother who lived in San Francisco.

After we arrived on the Mainland, my sister joined us. My mother moved us to Berkeley and she found a job as a nurse at Alta Bates Hospital.

When she was growing up in Harbin, Manchuria, the University of California had a local reputation of being a great university. So we moved to Berkeley to a house at 1521 Berkeley Way. We purchased a house closer to the hospital, at 2501 Prince Street, just across the street from Alta Bates. I had exciting experiences growing up in Berkeley and that's where we were when the War ended.

Shortly after the War there was an international gathering in San Francisco to celebrate the end of the War and to discuss the future. This led to the founding of the United Nations. When that conference came to a close, they wanted to have some sort of an artistic document. So, the United Nations Charter was printed at the University of California which had the necessary printing facilities.

I found it curious that my participation in World War II started at the very beginning while I listened to the broadcast of the attack at Pearl Harbor and, the document that formally ended the war was created while I was there in Berkeley.

I finished grammar school at Jefferson School, went to Willard Junior High School, then Berkeley High School, and entered the University of California.

*My professional life followed earning a degree in Forestry from the University of California in 1958. As a graduate of the ROTC program, I served a three year tour of active duty with the Army, initially at a Niki missile defense battery in the state of Maine, Loring Air Force Base, including participating on various Army rifle teams. After that, I worked for the Division of Forestry on the island of Maui, Hawaii. I then served as Forestry Conservation Officer of the Trust Territory of the Pacific Islands, formed by the United Nations at the close of World War II. This huge area of the Pacific Ocean covered virtually all of Micronesia. My home was at the Palau islands, where the battle of Peleliu island was fought.*

*I later returned to the University of California at the beginning of its Natural Reserves System (NRS), addressing the needs that natural areas were being taken over by development. In what amounted to a nature conservancy, I was the first field representative of the NRS. Thus, I was able to return to Berkeley where, as a student, I was active in the Cal Marching Band, ending my final year in school as the Drum Major of the Marching Band.*

*Adjusting to life on the Mainland was time consuming and it wasn't until high school that I learned for the first time, about the internment of the mainland Japanese. This shocked me and caught me totally off guard.*

# Too Young to Serve,
# Old Enough to Observe

## Patrick Crowley

I was born the year that
Franklin D. Roosevelt was elected
President. That meant that I was
nine years old when the Japanese
attacked Pearl Harbor and 13 when
the War concluded.

The years before and during
World War II were spent in
Southern California, first growing

up in Coronado, California, followed by years in San Jacinto,
San Diego, and El Cajon. I had arrived in Coronado on my
fourth birthday February 15, 1936. Coronado was in the heart
of San Diego Bay, immediately adjacent to the North Island
Naval Air Station. In fact, at four I met two children of naval
aviators who became my oldest and best friends well into
adult life. The Navy was a constant presence in San Diego
which earned the city the title of "Navy Town USA." Units
of the Pacific Fleet lay at anchor throughout the Bay with
destroyers and submarines tied up next to tenders at
permanent moorings in the Bay. North Island was the home
of many of the Navy's aircraft carriers.

In the pre-War period, officers did not wear their
uniforms when off duty. My friends' fathers were readily
identified, even in civilian attire, by their sun and wind burned

faces with white around their eyes from the goggles they wore. The Navy's planes of the era were open cockpit. In uniform, they were further distinct from the rest of the Navy in wearing Aviation Green uniforms with brown shoes. Surface Navy referred to aviators as "the Brown Shoe Navy."

With San Diego as the major West Coast base of the Navy, a build-up of the Navy was becoming apparent. Even before talk of the United States entering the war in Europe, Great Britain, to bolster their navy against the threat of German submarines, acquired 50 World War I destroyers that were moth-balled in San Diego in exchange for bases in various British Caribbean islands.

I had been living with my grandparents while still in grammar school. My grandfather spent many evenings next to the large console radio in the living room listening to the news. I sat near him much of the time and heard such broadcasters such as H.V. Kaltenborn and Gabriel Heatter discussing the gathering war clouds in Europe. Although he made his living as an automobile repair garage owner, he was intensely interested in politics and world affairs. While an ardent critic of our President, he, unlike too many people in the country, predicted a drift of Europe into a war that we in the United States would not be able to avoid.

While there was little public talk of US involvement in the war, there were signs that the United States was gearing up its military with the goal of greater preparedness. Across the Bay in San Diego, the aircraft company Consolidated-Vultee Aircraft was producing military aircraft. The PBY patrol seaplane was already in production for our Navy. In addition, in early 1941, B-24 bombers, also built by Consolidated, were seen in the skies with Royal Air Force rondels on wings and fuselages.

In 1939, when many Americans were not paying attention, war broke out in Europe with the invasion of Poland by Germany on September 1, 1939. France and England declared war, and a relatively calm period followed, during which the United Kingdom began gearing up for war, their seriousness signaled by electing a war government headed by Winston Churchill, who had long warned the West of an impending war. I clearly recall sitting with my grandfather by the radio when either Gabriel Heatter or H.V. Kaltenborn made reference to a popular song being played in England entitled "the White Cliffs of Dover. His comment was to the effect that "there will be bluebirds over the white cliffs of Dover, *Hell!,* There'll be buzzards."

An added indicator of things to come came when my mother, who had divorced my father when I was very young, began dating Deane Raine, who was attending the Ryan School of Aeronautics at Lindbergh Field in San Diego. Upon his graduation, he would become my step-father. He was hired to train pilots for the then-Army Air Corps.

After he married my mother, we joined him at Ryan Field in Hemet, California in rural Riverside County. All over the country, I was to learn later, similar airfields became the home of primary training for aviators. Our new family settled into a home some distance from the field, due to the housing impact of moving a major facility into a small farming town of Hemet. Our house was located near Gilman Hot Springs where I was enrolled in San Jacinto Elementary School, which was the closest school.

While living near Gilman Hot Springs, Deane took advantage of the golf course immediately across the highway from our house. He asked if I would care to caddy for him, and I quickly accepted. He reduced the number of clubs in his bag to accommodate his nine-year-old stepson.

Sundays were his golf days and on a bright Sunday morning we were completing the first 9 holes of the Gilman Hot Springs Golf Course. We stopped at a caddy shack for refreshment, and the attendant had the radio on. While we were standing there, the program was interrupted with an announcement that the United States Pacific Fleet in Pearl Harbor was under attack by naval air forces of the Japanese.

Over time, the cadet contingent at Hemet increased in size, the school expanding with more military personnel. Soon Ryan brought in PT-18 Stearman biplanes to supplement the Ryan PT-22 trainers originally in use. With the expansion, my step-father's brother Harry Raine was hired as a ground school instructor.

In my elementary school we were encouraged to buy Saving Stamps which were pasted into small booklets and, when full, was converted into a Twenty-Five Dollar Savings Bond. Despite the increased activity at Ryan Field, the war still seemed remote to this rural farming area.

What helped to make it more personal for me was when I was recruited by my fifth-grade teacher Helen Shields to assist her as a volunteer aircraft spotter. We were assigned to a location along Highway 79 connecting to Riverside to the north. A small tower had been constructed on an uphill slope from the highway. Equipped with a roof, plywood walls and plywood counter, the tower had an open side facing northwest. The only equipment was a telephone. I don't recall any restroom facilities, but with short assigned hours perhaps it was felt unnecessary.

Our duty hours were several days a week after school. Mrs. Shields would take me in her car to the site. We were provided with a log to record sightings with details. I had been chosen because, despite my age, I had extensive knowledge of aircraft having grown up around airplanes.

My first opportunity to employ my knowledge came when we sighted a bomber flying toward March Field to our north. Our telephone line was connected to the Filter Center located in Santa Ana. Mrs. Shields allowed me to call in the sighting. I stated our location, our names and the time of the sighting. I proceeded to report the sighting of a Boeing B-17G four-engined bomber flying at several thousand feet and headed on a northeasterly course. The person at the other end of the line abruptly corrected me asking me not to try to identify the aircraft other than stating the number of engines, wing location and features such as a single tail or twin tail. I explained that I recognized the plane as a B-17G because of its chin gun turret, a feature not appearing on earlier models of the bomber. In retrospect, I suppose the people at the center were dealing mostly with civilians who would not know one aircraft type over another, explaining their request for generic rather than specific information. At our location, fairly far inland, the majority of spottings were of primary training planes from Ryan Field in Hemet approximately fifteen miles away.

As the War progressed, there were many changes at Ryan Field. One which directly affected our family occurred when the commanding officer of the Air Corps contingent at Ryan Field was given orders to join the 20th Air Force in China. When Major Wayne Dooley left, his wife Jean and young daughter moved to her parent's home in San Diego. Not having a place for her Steinway Concert Grand piano, she left it temporarily with us. It was a wonderful opportunity for my mother to play the piano and for me to start lessons.

Reports were returning on the tremendous losses of pilots in the American bombing campaign against Germany. Deane, still a civilian, joined the Army Air Corps. He was sent to Tennessee where he received his officer's training, graduating as a Flight Officer Army Service Pilot. His initial assignment was to fighter transition training. There he was checked out in all the Air Corp's inventory of fighter aircraft. The only exception was the Lockheed P-38 Lightning, as he judged it to be an unsafe airplane.

He spent a number of months ferrying fighters from their respective factories to delivery point around the country. His favorite was the Bell P-39 Airacobra, followed by the Bell P-63 Supercobra as it came into production. He would fly the planes from upper New York State either to Great Falls, Montana, or, in some instances, to Fairbanks, Alaska. These planes were delivered to the Soviet Air Force, a favorite because of the .37 mm cannon that fired through the propeller shaft of these planes. It made a particularly good weapon against German tanks.

Deane had many opportunities to meet with the Russian pilots. The better English speakers could fly into Great Falls; otherwise, they flew to Fairbanks where Russian speakers manned the control tower. In conversations with the Russians, many would state that Americans were short-sighted in sending these fighters to Russia, as they considered the plane superior to any flown by the Americans. When too much liquor flowed, some of the Russians revealed that these same planes would be used against the United States after Russia defeated Germany. It was a wake-up call and a premonition of the Cold War to come.

In time, Deane moved on to multi-engine training in preparation for flying transports in the Air Transport Command. Before he received orders overseas, he flew some trips delivering aircraft such as the Douglas A-20, as well as several trips in the Pacific. My mother and I were with him after his first leave where, in Long Beach, California, he picked up his plane from the Douglas factory. A Cadillac convertible with the top down parked alongside. The occupant, with his aviator dark glasses and a snappy tailored uniform, got out of the car. I identified him immediately as Major Clark Gable.

Deane spoke of a particular trip flying a Curtiss C-46 loaded with five-gallon jerry cans of aviation fuel to a Pacific island. Being a heavy smoker, this was hard for him. Considering the flammability of his cargo, he used snuff to satisfy his nicotine habit. On that trip, he had a recently-commissioned navigator. Well into the trip, the navigator announced to Deane that he had made an error in his calculations and wasn't sure of their position. Considering the vast expanses of the Pacific and the number of flyers that were lost during the war when they couldn't find their destinations, this was not good news. Fortunately, as a pilot with many flying hours in single-seat aircraft, Deane was a competent navigator. He had been tracking their course and he was able to direct the navigator's attention to a spot on the horizon which ended up being their desired destination. When they landed, the Marines did not yet have total control of the island. Deane brought me a souvenir of a Japanese rifle shell casing that was still hot when he retrieved it.

Following that trip, Deane was sent to North Africa where he began a stint flying C-47 and C-46 cargo planes from North Africa to the Middle East and ultimately to India, Burma, and China. He would remain on this route for most of the duration.

While he was with ATC, my mother and I moved to 49th Street in San Diego with Major Dooley's wife Jean and their young daughter Marilyn. Thanksgiving of 1944 arrived. Jean and Marilyn had family in San Diego that they would spend the day with. My mother assumed that Deane, being overseas, would likely miss a normal Thanksgiving feast. She decided that we would have Boston baked beans and Boston Brown Bread, both out of cans. It was pretty depressing, but we shared our meal in the spirit of sacrifice. In Deane's next letter, he spoke of the lavish Thanksgiving he experienced at an airbase in India, complete with turkey, ham, roasts of local cattle and all the trimmings.

I was still living with my grandparents in El Cajon when the war ended with VJ Day. My buddy Greg Black was visiting at the grove when the news broke. Equipped with my plastic Boy Scout bugle, we bussed to downtown San Diego to join in the raucous celebration at Horton Plaza with thousands of sailors, Marines, and civilians.

Shortly after the War, Deane returned to us in El Cajon. He stayed with us while he sorted out his return to civilian life. Many of his classmates from Ryan School of Aeronautics ended up as test pilots, airline pilots or crop dusters. As test pilots for Ryan, several of them died in crashes of the Ryan XFR-1 Fireball fighter. The plane, with a reciprocating engine in the nose and a jet engine in the tail, was designed to operate off the Navy's aircraft carriers addressing the problems of slow acceleration of jet aircraft. The plane failed to meet the Navy's requirements for duty with the Fleet. One thing that Deane did not want was to be an airline pilot, or as he referred to the position as "bus drivers," which is what he was for the Air Transport Command.

Other family members also served during the War. My Aunt Kathleen trained bomber crews assigned to the B-24 bomber. Her husband Charles Newman II, from a West Texas cattle ranching family, entered Naval Intelligence after graduating from Texas School of Mines in El Paso, Texas. Initially, he was stationed near the Mexican border in Loredo, Texas, because of his fluency in Spanish. He was later transferred to London, England. It was rumored that the transfer was a result of the fact that his cousin was married to the head of the Mexican Communist Party. In London, he was able to participate in the theater scene in his off-duty hours.

My birth father spent the War years after being drafted as an instructor in the ROTC Program at Stanford University. He and my step-mother lived in a duplex quarters overlooking the Golden Gate Bridge in the San Francisco Presidio.

The only other family member to serve was my Uncle Dee Tilley. Joining up while still in high school, he trained at Catalina Island to become a member of the Merchant Marine. He made a single round trip on the Matson liner *SS Lurline*, converted to a troopship. His one trip was to transport members of the Timberwolf Division to France after the D Day Invasion. He resigned to return to high school. After graduation, he enlisted in the Air Force with the intention of making the military his career. He was the only career military person in our family until my mother remarried years later to a Naval Officer who served in the Pacific, where he was wounded and was retired from the Navy as a Commander.

My contributions to the War effort were the usual home-front activities with Savings Stamps and, as a Boy Scout, participating in scrap drives, and at home, delivering bacon fat to our local grocer in exchange for meat stamps. I participated in a program making identification model airplanes for the military and did my tour as a volunteer aircraft-spotter working with my Fifth Grade teacher.

*At the end of World War II, I continued with my education, still on the move. I attended five elementary schools, four high schools and four colleges/universities including Earlham College, San Diego State College, the University of California, Berkeley, graduating with a BA in History (1956) from San Diego State College and a Master of City Planning degree (1972) from San Diego State University. I became a licensed architect and later a city planner for an interlude before returning to architectural practice. During my professional career, we lived in Berkeley, Carmel, San Diego, Gilroy, and Carmel (again) and retired in San Diego. My wife Ann and I moved to Sacramento in 2011 to be near family, moving to URC in March 2017.*

# Overheard and Never Forgotten

## Amy Moore

When the war began during the school year of 1941-42, I was a sophomore. Then I sat down to what proved to be a sobering awareness of one aspect of the cost of war that we hear little of. News reports and historical records of the dollar costs and battlefield casualties abound. Not recorded, and seldom mentioned, are the sacrifices made by those of us who stayed behind, armed with tender hope, fervent prayer, and little else.

Early in that school year, I went alone to have lunch in the school cafeteria—alone because I had no friend to go with, as we had come to live in that town a scant 6 or 7 days before the school year began. I looked for a vacant seat anywhere at all and sat down at the first one I could find.

Several girls already sitting there were actively engaged in conversation; they did not notice me, but I could not help noticing them, nor overhearing their conversation. They spoke in raised voices so they could hear each other over the overwhelming din of other conversations.

Their conversation was about a missing ring, a ring they were accustomed to seeing every day. The fervency of their engagement with one another suggested that this ring was more than just a trinket picked up at the county fair. No trinket, the missing ring was a gold ring with a diamond setting worn as recently as the week before by the girl who seemed to be at the center of the conversation. It was an engagement ring, *her* engagement ring, given to her not long before by Bud, who had proposed to her the evening of his graduation in May, enlisted in the army one week later, and was now overseas.

Questions about the ring flew fast and furious at the girl who was no longer wearing it. "You're not wearing the ring?" "No." "How come? You're not giving it, back are you?" "No, of course not." She would never give it back, no matter what.

"Why aren't you wearing it?" She couldn't. It was all over, she said, and she was heartbroken; she said she just couldn't wear it now or ever, because it was too much a part of the love she felt for him, and the promise they had made to each other a promise they could not keep. She said she couldn't even keep it either. She didn't have it any more, she told them as tears rolled down her cheeks and sobs interrupted her speaking.

"Well, if you're not giving it back and you're not keeping it…what?" She told them she had gone back to the place by the river where they had gone together when he had proposed to her. She had sat there for a time, turning the ring around her finger as she recalled the joy she felt just being with him, the racing in her heart as he proposed, the awkwardness they both felt as he fumbled placing it on her finger, the unforgettable hug and the quiet exhilaration she felt then, wrapped in the embrace of his arms around her and her arms around him. As the reality of knowing none of that could ever be experienced again, she had taken the ring off her finger and thrown it into the middle of the river.

"Why?" Bud would not be coming back to her.

"Oh, you don't know that!" they insisted. "What's happened that you think that? If anything, he loves you even more than you love him. Don't you know that?" "Yes," she knew that.

She explained what had just made the certainties more painful to bear than his going away was that she had just learned Bud's name had been added to the list of casualties as

KIA—Killed in Action. She, and all her friends there that noontime, finished their lunch hour, sobbing without restraint.

The bell rang. We were all expected to return, as always, to our classrooms. But it was not "as always" that day, or for many days that came afterward for them. Not for me, either, who had overheard and have not yet forgotten, that she, too, was a casualty, unlisted, uncounted, seldom spoken of, or even recognized as a "casualty of war." One of how many?

We don't know.

*I was the daughter of a mining engineer with an emphasis in geologic exploration. I grew up in mining towns in Utah, Colorado and New Mexico. At 17 I entered the University of Colorado earning a BS in Nursing in 1948. In 1951 I married Robert Moore who had a position with the Medicare program of the Social Security Administration. We settled in Baltimore, MD where we had three boys and three girls.*

*I worked in a wide variety of positions all relating to nursing and teaching. After retirement, Bob and I moved to Cottonwood, AZ where he could play golf the year round. Bob died soon after. I then moved to Woodland, CA to be near a daughter who lives in Davis. I met and married John Green who lived in Davis. He died in 2007. Through my church I came to know the late URC resident Nancy DuBois and later became a reader for Nancy on Saturday afternoons. That experience gave me an inside look at some of the advantages that characterize URC and led to my becoming a resident in 2016.*

# My World War II Memories
## Georgia Paulo, Civilian

December 7, 1941. I was 10 years old at the time, living in Venice, California. I have a vivid mental picture of the setting when we heard the radio inform us of the Japanese bombing of Pearl Harbor. Though at ten years of age I didn't understand the significance of the news. I could tell by the obvious emotions of my parents this was an important life-changing event.

My Dad soon became a Block Warden in our residential neighborhood. Blackout curtains were installed on all of the outside windows. Part of his duty was to patrol the neighborhood to be sure that all residents had installed and were using the blackout curtains so that no light was visible outside at night. Sometimes I walked with him on his patrol.

I also remember nights when we had air-raid drills. Venice, California, is close to the Pacific Ocean, and there was fear of Japanese air attacks. Probably not the smartest thing to do if Japanese planes had actually come, but I liked to stand in  front of  our apartment complex  by the street and watch the crisscrossing searchlight beams, bright in the night sky. It was entertainment. TV was not yet on the scene. We huddled near the static-riddled Philco radio housed in an overly-large wooden cabinet in the living room to hear the latest wartime developments.

During the Great Depression, my parents had been forced to leave farming in Nebraska where they were going deeper and deeper in debt. We moved to California. My uncle, who was a lineman for Associated Telephone Company in Santa Monica, CA, got my Dad a job paying 35 cents per hour digging trenches for buried phone cables. Income from a steady paying job was a big draw. I am an only child, so I and all the earthly possessions that would fit in the 1929 Buick sedan were packed for the trip. No overnight stops could be afforded, so my parents took turns driving from the Nebraska farm to the California home of the generous aunt and uncle we lived with until my folks got on their financial feet.

In addition to Dad's paying job my mother worked as a housekeeper for the Bullock family who owned the merry-go-round on Santa Monica Pier, a ride called the Dragon Slide and several other popular pier entertainments.

On weekends my Dad worked at the Dragon Slide. Sometimes I went along to watch. The ride required a long hike up to the top of the tall wooden structure. There the rider was helped into sitting up in a sort of sleeping bag-type fabric case to slide down the spiral wooden trough to the bottom. Many climbed right back up to the top to wait their turn to slide down again. Too daring for me, but I loved to use my free ride card on the merry-go-round. The last I knew, the carousel is still on the Santa Monica Pier. It was used in the 1973 Paul Newman/Robert Redford movie "The Sting" as if it were in Chicago.

As was standard at the time, money was sent back to the people in Nebraska until all debts were cleared. We then moved from living with my Mom's brother and his wife and were on our own. At the time of the Pearl Harbor bombing, my parents were managing a rental complex named Porter Court in Venice, California. This was a group of four duplex units (eight apartments), one-story stucco, red-tile-roofed units facing a central grassy courtyard with eight single-car garages lined along the alley at back. My Dad now worked in maintenance at the Standard Oil Refinery, probably making more than 35 cents per hour. Also, he took care of the apartment grounds and repairs as needed. My Mom collected the rents, took care of the banking, and kept the books for the owner of the rentals. Our apartment was a one-bedroom unit. My "bedroom" was a Murphy bed in a closet behind two large wooden doors on one wall of the living room.

At the time of the bombing attack on Pearl Harbor, my parents were in the process of buying a house that was under construction in Santa Monica. This was to be the first property owned by them. With all necessary materials going to wartime needs, it became very difficult to secure the goods needed to finish construction on the new hillside two-bedroom, one-bath, single-car-garage home. After many delays, we moved in. My Dad got a job as a riveter at nearby Douglas Aircraft. My Mom became cafeteria manager at the John Adams Junior High School that I attended.

We had a very large backyard. The farming instincts kicked in, and we raised chickens for the eggs and Sunday supper. Rabbits and turkeys were also part of the menu. We would have had a large vegetable garden anyhow, but because of the war, we got credit for having a Victory Garden. My picture as a 12 year-old appeared in the *Santa Monica Evening Outlook* with the caption indicating that I won one of four War Stamp prizes out of 379 Victory Gardens in Santa Monica in May 1944.

Since our home on Ashland Avenue was in the flight path to Douglas Aircraft, an Army barrage balloon/observation tower took over what had been an empty residential lot on top of a hill just up our street. My

Mom and I often delivered plates of homemade cookies to the grateful army men stationed there.

Because of the importance in the war effort of the Santa Monica Douglas Aircraft Plant, there was a fear of a Japanese air attack. The entire plant spent World War II shielded by a sophisticated camouflage structure. Designed by architects with the aid of Warner Bros movie set designers, a tension-compression structure covered the entire mile-long plant. Made of burlap, netting and with trees fashioned from green-dyed chicken feathers, we were told that from above, the area seemed to be a continuation of our Sunset Park residential neighborhood. Cars continued to drive on the roads under the netting. As a decoy, a dummy aircraft plant was erected nearby, but away from the actual production facility. Tanker trucks sprayed green paint on the runway to simulate a green field. Almost five million square feet of chicken wire was stretched across 400 very tall poles to disguise the aircraft plant. The tallest hangar was made to look like a gently sloping hillside neighborhood. We were very impressed. It probably was good fortune that the movie-set designers of Hollywood were not far from Santa Monica and the essential airplane plant.

As was very typical at the time, my mother was accustomed to canning the bounty from our garden and fruit trees. In my wartime souvenirs, I came across the form required to buy a five-pound bag of sugar for home canning. We Must Get Along With Less Sugar This Year Because—

---

WE MUST GET ALONG WITH LESS SUGAR THIS YEAR BECAUSE—

1. Military needs are high. Each soldier actually consumes twice as much sugar a year as the average civilian now receives.
2. Ships which otherwise might be bringing sugar into the United States are hauling supplies to the battle fronts.
3. Manpower is scarce at sugar refineries and shipping ports.
4. Beet sugar production last year was 500,000 tons short, making the stock of sugar smaller for this year.
5. Last year many people over-applied for canning sugar. We used so much sugar that stocks at the beginning of this year were abnormally low.

DO NOT APPLY FOR MORE SUGAR THAN YOU ACTUALLY NEED FOR HOME CANNING — HELP MAKE OUR WAR SHORT SUGAR SUPPLIES LAST ALL YEAR

During the war everyone willingly did their part. We adapted to War Ration Books for coffee, sugar, meat, shoes, gasoline, and tires. My parents' "A" sticker allowed us to have four gallons of gas per week. Sunday pleasure drives were given up "for the duration." My Dad had a cigarette ration card. My mother filled a metal coffee can with bacon grease, which was taken to our local meat market for meat coupons. Yes, coffee came in metal cans with a small metal "key" attached. This key had a slot in it that fit into the metal strip on the can lid. Once the key was inserted you could twist off the top of the can and release the sealed-in, wonderful aroma of a new supply of ground coffee. I wasn't allowed to drink coffee then, but I enjoyed the task of opening a new can of coffee to savor that wonderful aroma.

**LOS ANGELES CITY SCHOOLS**
VIERLING KERSEY, Superintendent

## Patriotic Thrift Creed

**Patriotism**
I believe in the UNITED STATES OF AMERICA.
I believe that her progress depends upon the INDUSTRY and THRIFT of her people.

**Punctuality**
Therefore, I will devote my time to worthwhile activities and SAVE TIME by being punctual.

**Physical Training**
I will PRESERVE my HEALTH, because without it I have less earning power.

**Conservation**
I will CONSERVE MATERIALS, because materials cost money.

**Thrift**
I will SAVE my MONEY, because saving leads to security, helpfulness, and happiness. I will buy DEFENSE STAMPS or BONDS to help make my country SECURE.

I WILL DO ALL THESE THINGS FOR THE WELFARE OF THE UNITED STATES OF AMERICA

Signed: *Georgia Lee Dodendorf*

Another of my wartime projects was to knead the bubble of yellow food coloring encased in the see-through package of very white oleomargarine until the color was evenly distributed. The end result was that the oleomargarine looked more like real butter, but it never tasted like real butter. School-age children were encouraged to sign a "Patriotic Thrift Creed" and buy defense savings stamps and bonds. My completed card shows that in 1942 I purchased $50 in defense bonds. To quote the card: "Stand up for your country. It is standing up for you!"

*My career after high school included meeting Bill Paulo while attending Santa Monica Community College. His career in education culminated 42 years later as founder and professor emeritus of the La Verne University doctoral program in educational management. Five children were born followed by six grandchildren. I worked as a secretary for Douglas Aircraft, Riverside County Hospital and Fullerton junior high schools. We had homes in*  *Santa Monica, El Segundo, Riverside, Fullerton, Santa Barbara, Lake Arrowhead and Lake Wildwood.*

*After 22 years in a home on Lake Wildwood Golf Course we moved to URC after much investigation and touring, moving in 2010. Shortly thereafter, Bill suffered a fatal heart attack. After much support from residents, I married widower Ray Vincent in August of 2011.*

# War Worker

## Sonia Blostein Pollack

My Name is Sonia Blostein Pollack. On December 7, 1941, I was a high school freshman in Athens, PA (a small northern Pennsylvania town where I was born in 1927.) I was living with my parents and younger sister. My mother, who was born in New York City, was a veteran of WW I, having served in the Navy as a Yeoman Female in Washington, D.C. I have pictures of her in her uniform, and the victory parade after the war.

I was at the local soda shop on that Sunday afternoon, and I don't remember if I heard about the attack there, or from my parents when I got home that afternoon. They had been listening to the radio, and I had never heard of Pearl Harbor and wanted to know where it was. My mother (who was ill) was intensely interested in the news until her death 12 days later.

We collected aluminum, cooking fat; used ration books for meat, soap, sugar, gasoline; rolled bandages; served coffee, sandwiches to the Navy recruits on their way to Sampson Naval Training base on lake Seneca, NY from Penn Station in New York City. The rail station was in Sayre, PA, 2 miles from my home.

Around 6 boys from our high school class enlisted before graduation. There were about fifty-seven in the graduating class in May 1945. All during the war there were weekly assemblies in our school auditorium; during D-Day, on President Roosevelt's death, and other occasions, we heard radio broadcasts of the events.

After graduation until VJ Day I worked night shift at the Eclipse Machine Division of Bendix Aviation Corp, where fuel pumps for B-29 bombers were being manufactured. The plant was in Elmira Heights, NY, and had made coaster brakes for bicycles before the war.

Bernard Pollack, whom I married in 1949, was born in Detroit in 1920. He was schooled in Detroit until the 9th grade, when his widowed mother returned to western Pennsylvania with her four children to be near her family. He graduated from Tarentum High School in 1938, attended Forestry School until 1940, and he worked in Oil City, PA.

He and his younger brother enlisted in the Army and entered service 9/12/42. He was discharged 2/11/46. He was an artillery mechanic (anti-aircraft) and served as cadre in the U.S. until he was shipped to England in a convoy 12/26/44. (He said they spent Christmas in NY harbor because it would have looked bad for them to leave on that day.) He arrived in England 1/7/45. While in England he and his bother, who had been hospitalized after the Normandy invasion, met in London on a brief leave—both returned to their posts early, because of the buzz bombs saturating London.

At some point, his unit was sent to Le Havre, traveled by train (40 and 8 from WW I) to Aix and then shipped out of Marseilles through the Panama Canal to New Guinea, where there was staging for the Japanese invasion. Shortly after their arrival the war ended and they were sent to the Philippines, There, his unit was accepting jeeps that were being stored until they were eventually dumped in Manila Bay.

On 1/12/46 he received orders to report for return to the U.S. They stopped in Hawaii for supplies and then returned to New York through the Panama Canal. He often joked that he spent more time at sea than many who served in the Navy. He said they were very well fed on the ship (a large passenger vessel.)

Sometime after his discharge he worked at either Fort Meade, or Aberdeen Proving Grounds, and then received an invitation to return to Penn State to continue his education. We met there in the summer of 1948 and we were married in May 1949. He had switched his major to Horticulture and was working in the experimental plots there. Using his GI Bill he completed his undergraduate work, MS, and his doctorate in 1951.

He often said that the GI Bill benefits were the most wonderful gift he could have received.

He was on the faculty at Rutgers University and the Cooperative Extension of the Department of Agriculture in NJ from 1960 until retirement in 1985. He died July 14, 2014.

*After Bernie retired in 1985, we moved to San Diego to be near our daughter and first grandchild. Bernie became a specialist in repairing antique industrial time recorders, and we took two "clock tours" in England. I learned to quilt, play bridge, and do counted cross-stitch, but loved mysteries most of all. I was "back-up care" for my grandchildren.*

*Bernie died in 2014, after having thirty years after open-heart surgery. Since my mother died at 41, I never expected this long life I am experiencing! I moved to URC in May 2016 from Oceanside, California.*

# Other Paths

# Second World War in Scotland

## Deanne Buchan

I was born in Scotland in 1938 and so was only 3 years old when the Second World War was declared.

I have recorded here a few memories during not only the war years but also the recovery in the post-war years which in many ways was more difficult than during the War.

Certain things/events I remember vividly:

My father's photograph on the mantelpiece in his army uniform in the Libyan Desert,

Our gas masks in the sitting room cupboard, which were scary looking when one put them on, and a bucket of eggs in the basement: my step-mother used a preserving solution that sealed the eggs so they would keep and not go bad. This bucket we were warned not to touch it or we would be "burned." Because I had no idea what this solution was, I was deathly scared to go near it. I don't know if we ever ate the eggs; they seemed to stay there for an awfully long time.

At the beginning of the War all the houses on my grandmother's street were surrounded by iron railings. These were taken out to be used ostensibly for armament manufacture. I remember jumping from one iron stump to another—they were part of the landscape, and I don't think we had any idea that they were railing stumps, because the railings were never replaced.

The blackout was mandatory in all the houses. In our house, the bedrooms had cardboard cut to the window shape and put in place each evening. The family room and sitting room had heavy drapes, as there was no air conditioning; it could get very stuffy in the house. Flashlights (we called torches) were shaded so light would only be cast on the pavement/sidewalk in front of us. There was no curfew; however, people did not venture out at night, and all able-bodied souls were "away at war."

In 1941, 1942, 1943 school-age children were evacuated out of the cities. I was too young, but I remember thinking how exciting! However, there were horrid tales of child abuse that came out after the war.

Liberty bodices: we had to wear them to keep warm in the winter. Today I am amused by the name "liberty bodice," but they were undergarments of thick padded cotton that was practically bulletproof.

Coupon books: for everything including clothing and shoes. Garments marked with "utility labels" used fewer coupons but were of poor quality. I remember disliking the utility label without knowing why. All our underwear had utility labels.

An aunt, a gifted seamstress, made my cousin Nina and me party dresses out of net curtain material. Not that we went to parties but we would imagine how we would dance wearing these dresses "after the war." We did not take into account that we would be grown out of them!

In 1943 my step-mother and her sisters decided that spending time at the coast for the summer was safer than staying in Glasgow, where the bombing of the shipyards was in full swing. I don't know that Girvan, our destination, was any safer than further up the Clyde in Glasgow; nevertheless, it felt safer, and it was at the seaside, always an attraction to us kids. We were too young to appreciate how the farm where we stayed relieved the deprivations of war. We enjoyed fresh milk, eggs, chicken, and pork sausages, along with an abundance of vegetables and fruits from the smallholding garden. How hard the Kerrs, owners of the smallholding, worked! Mrs. Kerr looked after the dairy and the animals and tended the vegetable garden. And for extra income, a large local farm employed Mr. Kerr. It also employed many Poles who had escaped from Warsaw in 1941. I imagine we gave over our coupon books to the Kerrs.

There was an American army base just up the road from the farm, and every so often big army trucks would thunder by. We kids would run out to the side of the road and yell, "Any gum chum?" and these obliging young lads would dig into their pockets and throw us sweets or whatever else they had. On one occasion we picked up a ball of darning wool, much to the distress of Aunty Tina (Nina's mum), who envisioned the soldier on the battlefield with holes in his socks.

What a far cry that place was from war-torn Europe! Only the passing of the American soldiers in their big trucks, the barrage balloons high in the sky, and the occasional plane overhead reminded us children that a war was going on.

*After the War at 17 I started nursing school and at twenty-two, had two degrees in general nursing and midwifery, practicing in Glasgow and London. Looking for adventure, at twenty-three I went to Aden in the Middle East where I was required to learn Arabic to treat the locals as well as employees of British Petroleum. After 18 months I found the social life too hectic at a locale which included members of the British Army, Air Force and Marines. My next stop was in North Borneo working in a government hospital in Kota Kinabalu. There I met my first husband and for 9 years lived in various locations in Malaysia and Singapore, and where our daughter was born. Business took us to New Zealand where I entered a second career in the theater and adopted our son. After three years my husband became severely ill and died. In 1978 I began a new*

*life in California with a new husband. Living near Mill Valley I pursued my theatrical career and was instrumental in the development of the Marin Theater Company. After six years my husband retired and we returned to California after a seven and half year stint in Houston, TX ,where I earned a BA in Theater Arts. We had started a small vineyard in Yolo County near Davis. My second husband passed away in 2010.*

*In 1997 I became very involved in NAMA (National Alliance of Mental Illness). I was trained by NAMI in the Family-to-Family program that helped families through education to cope with severe psychiatric disorders. I became one of the first trainers in Northern California for the program and ran it in Yolo County for 12 years. I moved to URC in 2013.*

# A Time That Lives in Infamy

## Joan Callaway

The day "that will live in infamy"—Pearl Harbor, Sunday morning, December 7, 1941. War declared! What did that mean to an almost eleven-year-old? It meant that my nineteen-year-old brother Bill, who had been attending Grays Harbor Junior College, immediately joined the Merchant Marine. I'm not sure why Bill chose the Merchant Marine over the Army, Navy or Marines. My best guess is that there had been a recruitment officer at the college, or perhaps it was because the pay was said to be good. Or maybe it was because one could get out immediately if it proved to be disappointing.

He quickly shipped out on the Star of Scotland, an old-time sailing vessel that had just been overhauled and put back in service. In years past, it had been used to carry supplies along the Pacific Coast and to Alaska, after which it had been retired to California where the beautiful old ship became an off-shore gambling casino.

The country was so ill-prepared for war that these kinds of ships were brought out of retirement to carry the supplies that were needed all over the world to fight the Germans and Japanese. Bill sailed on the Star of Scotland's first wartime voyage to Africa, carrying mostly lumber.

When war was declared, the family of my brother's college classmate of Japanese descent owned a radio store in Aberdeen. They were second-generation Americans, but this didn't seem to matter to the people who broke windows and virtually destroyed their store, fearing they were spies, radioing important information to the Japanese. The contents of their store were confiscated, the family losing everything they owned when they were taken away for the duration of the war "for their own protection" and incarcerated in a camp in Eastern Washington for the duration of the war.

We knew this family and how unfair it was, but I suppose much as the common people of Germany felt helpless to do anything about the "internment" in concentration camps, we were at a loss as to what we might do in Hoquiam. This happened to families like theirs all up and down the Coast.

Those of us who were left at home had some minor wartime preparations to make and a few challenges, too. Since we were living on the Pacific Coast–and very near the coast in Hoquiam, Washington–we had to black out our windows with heavy black curtains at night, so that no trace of lights could be seen from off the coastline, should there be Japanese submarines or planes out there.

Volunteers from every neighborhood, called "air raid wardens," patrolled each night to be sure no light could be seen from our houses. Every house had pails of sand, extra water, and flashlights in case of an attack. Eerie-sounding special air-raid sirens were installed in every community and tested regularly to be sure they worked properly. In addition to fire drills at school, we now practiced what we would do should there be an air raid, occasionally climbing under our desks for protection from ceilings that might cave in; other times we practiced evacuating to a special shelter that was eventually built.

It was a nerve-wracking time for everyone, especially for anyone who had family members in the service, particularly in foreign waters or lands. President Roosevelt's Fireside Chats and rationing made us all feel a part of the war effort though. Americans were asked to conserve everything – shared sacrifice.

Food Ration Stamps were instituted, perhaps more to help the people of our country to feel involved in the war effort than because of actual need for rationing, I suspect. Some people were caught hoarding food "just in case."

Recycling was born during this time when with the government's urging, saving aluminum cans meant more armaments for soldiers. We were encouraged to conserve and recycle metal, paper, and rubber. Communities banded together to hold scrap-iron drives. Many people planted "Victory Gardens" as a way to aid in the war effort.

I remember as if it were yesterday the day my mother arrived at my school, calling me out of class to tell me my brother's ship had been sunk. My mother wanted to be the one to tell me before someone else reported hearing on the radio that the Star of Scotland had been sunk by a German submarine on its return from Africa. The headlines in our local paper read "Bill Campbell, local boy, among missing."

As it turned out, the Captain and three boatloads of stores had been taken from the ship before the rest of the crew was allowed to man a couple of lifeboats with no navigational equipment. The first mate fell overboard during the transfer of the lifeboats to the water and quickly fell behind the ship a couple of hundred feet. Search as they might, they were unable to find him; he was the only man lost.

The sub came alongside, and my brother remembered being relieved to find it was German rather than Japanese. By this time, the Japanese already had a reputation of being not only less friendly, but apt to "take no prisoners," shooting them all.

Realizing that his inexperienced crew could never make land without either him or his First Mate, the Captain finally persuaded the German submarine commander to allow him to return to the lifeboat to try to navigate to land; he promised that he would never command another ship against Germany.

With inadequate supplies for the 17 men and such a long impending journey, they set off. The Germans allowed them 35 gallons of water, a case of apricots, two cases of sweetened condensed milk, 2½ cases of evaporated milk, a tank of sea biscuits, four 5-pound loaves of liver cheese, a couple of tins of butter, and a four-gallon tin of bread.

They headed toward what they hoped would be land. After what seemed like forever and with their supplies almost depleted, they sighted land. They had navigated safely 1100 miles to finally land at the Santa Martha lighthouse on the African coast exactly eighteen days after the ship had sunk.

It was a sad, scary time for all the family waiting at home. It was a thirsty and hungry time of immobility and meager, strictly rationed food for the men on board the lifeboat. Bill was the youngest man on the crew, one of the few who could walk when they first landed.

After a leave to rest and recuperate from this ordeal, Bill was to continue in the service, eventually earning his First Mate license at the age of 24. After one last trip to Japan, he returned home in January of 1946, his final voyage.

After the war was over, the Captain received a letter from the sub commander: "Do you recall that although my orders were to take you prisoner, for the sake of your men, I allowed you to go free, and we shook hands saying that after the war, we might be friends? I shake your hands again and tell you that there is so little food here, and it is difficult to take care of my wife and children. Perhaps you could remember our friendship pledge."

Captain Flink sent a food package to the German to repay a wartime favor with the comment that "war is war and there were all kinds of men in it. He was a sailor."

Excerpts from ...*Invisible to the Eye: The First Forty Years* by Joan Snodgrass Callaway, 2011

*I was born in Aberdeen, Washington, educated in a small two-room school then Lincoln High School in Tacoma, followed by Reed College and the University of Washington. In 1951, I married Glen Snodgrass, a boyfriend from high school and Reed College. Glen completed his education at UW while I stayed at home raising our five children. After completing an MPH degree at the University of California, Glen, on a U.S. Public Health grant, helped integrate Touro Infirmary in New Orleans. While there, I worked as the Director of Religious Education for a church that was fire-bombed during the Civil Rights movement. We returned to California when Glen assisted in the location of the next medical school for the University of California. He ended up as Assistant Dean for Administration of the new medical school at Davis. I worked at the Dean's Office-Agriculture as a secretary and speechwriter.*

*Disaster struck when our home burned and I lost Glen and one son. I survived as a widow raising four children through a variety of activities. I co-founded Bereavement Outreach learning the plight of families when one of them suffers from mental illness. This led to my co-founding the Yolo Community Care Continuum with services for the mentally ill.*

*On the fourth of July, 1976 I married Ed Callaway. After opening several women's clothing stores, I organized and managed an upscale consignment shop with a non-profit board to benefit 12 agencies serving the mental health needs of Yolo County. After being sidelined by knee and ankle surgery, I tutored young students in reading, as well as high school students in writing at home. I facilitated a memoir writing group and published* It's an Ill Wind *followed by a more autobiographical account of my first forty years entitled* Invisible to the Eye. *Ed and I moved to URC in 2013 where I continued to facilitate a memoir writing group of residents as well as writing and occasionally editing the URCADIAN, the URC monthly newsletter.*

# Waldport, Oregon, Civilian Public Service—Camp CPS 56

## Vladimir Dupree

I was born on September 22, 1920, to American parents who were living in Prague, Czechoslovakia. When I was 5, the family and I returned to Worthington, Ohio. Subsequently, I graduated from a John Dewey experimental high school and Oberlin College. I participated in sports and wrote that I was an all-American boy, but with one major difference—I followed my parents who were socialists and pacifists, engaging in strikes, protests, and marches on behalf of the disenfranchised. I was opposed to violence and war-making and was working for the Fellowship of Reconciliation in New York until I was drafted into the Civilian Public Service (CPS) as a Conscientious Objector, classified as IV-E, available for alternative service.

The CPS was a plan of service provided under the United States Selective Service and Training Act of 1940 for conscientious objectors who were unwilling to perform any kind of military service. Nearly 12,600 young men were assigned to CPS camps to perform "work of national importance." For the duration plus 6 months, the men worked 8 ½ hours a day, 6 days a week. The camps were run by the Peace Churches (Brethren Service Committee, American Friends Service Committee, and Mennonite Central Committee), which also provided room and board plus

$2.50/month. There were no fences around the camps. If a man were to walk out, he would be apprehended by the FBI.

Located in the Siuslaw National Forest camp #056, Waldport had been a Civilian Conservation Corp facility. During WW II, it was administrated by the Brethren as a CPS camp, and designated as a Fine Arts Camp, in that professional writers, artists, actors and musicians were assigned there. Although they worked 50 hours a week, they also staged plays, read plays, printed program folders and collections of plays, short stories, and poetry, hosted a concert series, and hand-printed books under the leadership of William Everson and the United Press.

Our Waldport CPS Camp 56 was composed of 96 individuals drafted for public service as conscientious objectors. We represented 31 different religious sects as well as a good number of agnostics and atheists. As members of the Fine Arts Group, we lived together in the front part of barrack #1, along with some 15 Jehovah's Witnesses in the back section.

Each morning those working under the supervision of the United States Forest Service assembled at 8 AM to be taken to work sites: road maintenance or building, tree planting, fire fighting, or trail  building  and  maintenance. Forest Service personnel trained and supervised us, and we worked in all kinds of weather. It rained frequently and the appropriate dress was limited. Our packaged lunch was prepared by the kitchen cooks. In rain, we struggled to eat quickly enough to avoid soggy sandwiches. Skilled men such as mechanics and plumbers did work related to their skills. I helped plant 1,800,000 trees by hand, scrambling over burned-out forests. We built and maintained trails and roads, fought forest fires. I also later became a cook and baker, night watchman, and Director of the Fine Arts Program.

I learned new skills as well as disciplined work, physical and mental, that occurred in all jobs. Collaboration with a variety of people and with a different history and cultural beliefs, was learned over time.

We learned from each other the necessary skills as well as the value of disciplined work. Political, religious and social issues got in the way at times, giving us opportunities to learn how to resolve issues: when liberals went on slow-down strikes, others of religious beliefs went the "second mile" by doing two shifts a day, causing feelings that needed repair, sometimes successful, sometimes not. It was a vibrant, fluid social system, providing opportunities for problem-solving and learning.

The forest service work for six days a week was only one area of my life. Work at night on Fine Arts projects opened new skills for me: typesetting and running the press for Bill Everson and others of the United Press. I came to value printing by hand as an art form, expanding my horizons in spirituality, intellectual interests, and a new appreciation of art and music. As in college, it was a new opportunity among dedicated artists to risk and learn, facing both success and failure.

All of this has led me to believe it would be useful for all 18-year-olds to serve our country in some form or another: in the military, hospitals, medical research, improving infrastructures, or firefighting, where we give 18-year-olds a way to democratize our culture and further their maturing by having a serious commitment to giving to others and to the U. S., not just be self-absorbed. All our work was dangerous, requiring that others were observant and available for help. Three men of the 96 were killed in accidents on the job.

Examples of the legacies of the Fine Arts Camp members is found in the paintings of Morris Graves, the poetry of William Everson, and the works of book designers and Adrian Wilson, who was awarded a "genius" award of $208,000 by the MacArthur Foundation in 1983.

Bill Everson, our spiritual leader, spoke for me when he wrote: "There are men here and they saw to the heart of the pure creative substance, the rock, and began cutting it, and they cut off layer after layer of incidentals, and they got to the heart of it, stripped it down, and made it shine. They made it shine in painting, in music, in drama, in hand-printing books, poetry, essays, and crafts and nothing else really matters, except when it came to another sphere – that of politics, and they made it shine, too."

The great years of my life lie there with it, providing endless renewal, and I'm proud of my part in it, proud to be one of the men. I salute Waldport in changing my life, opening new vistas, feelings, friendships, knowledge, skills, attitudes. I'm proud I learned and contributed to Forest Service Projects as well as being Executive Secretary of Fine Arts.

I again fell in love with the wildness of the sea in storms, the grandeur and beauty of forested mountains, Cape Perpetua, heartfelt talks with friends, Everson, James, Eshelman, Manche, Joyce, Adrian, Kermit, Kemper and my wife, Ibby.

Swimming year-round drew me with friends, as did catching a 35 lb. salmon running to deposit eggs, but soon appearing on the dinner table after I baked it for all 96 of us. Seeing sea lions swim along drew several of us to join in their honks. We adventured, experimented, setting my style of life and risking.

Fine Arts and the CPS Community life changed my professional career and passions: art collecting, music, more diverse reading, cooking, and baking, creating a sacred place in nature for our family and friends over 35 years. Like a stream, renewed in this case by visits with Waldport friends, I volunteered at Poetry Magazine, nationally a poetry leader; I wrote ads and was one of several "first readers."

I was not a significant figure as an artist while at CPS or later. Ibby's talent as an actress was our outstanding contribution. I devoured, learned, helped behind the scene administratively. This continued in my life but changed later as I grew more confident. However, my life continued its theme of "on the edge," much like Waldport's early "beat" environment. I am proud to have been a part of creating such a vibrant community of diverse talents, personalities committed to creation rather than destruction.

My brother Yeni had joined the medical corps as a non-combatant, I-A-O. Serving in the Philippines, he was killed by a Japanese bullet in 1944.

Elizabeth Taylor ("Ibby"), an actress, and I met at Oberlin, and in 1944 she came to Waldport to be married and to participate in theatrical productions. Upon my discharge, we had no money. In order to finance a three-year Ph. D. program at the University of Chicago Human Development program, we did domestic work and lived with the family of English professor S. I. Hayakawa. (I was able to use the skills I had developed in the Waldport kitchen.)

The Fine Arts Program was deeply marked by Everson's passions and demand for excellence in all endeavors. On the other hand, social and personal life was more chaotic. Parties were fueled by beer, the only alcohol we could afford. Manche and Ibby hitchhiked into Yachats for food and drink supplies. Every few months Ibby hitchhiked into Portland to wait tables at the Oregon Oyster Company Restaurant, bringing back money and other relationships. Joyce Lancaster left Bob Harvey to later marry Adrian Wilson, winner of the MacArthur "genius" award for hand-made books. Bob Harvey then married Manche, later to have two girls, while alcohol eventually took him to SF's skid row and death. Everson lost his wife to the benefit of Harmon, and Bess Earle left her marriage and one child.

When Ibby came to the Fine Arts Program at CPS as my wife in October 1944, she was very pleased to contribute her fine acting to the Theater Program. She built on her four years of being Oberlin College's best actress. Experienced directors were available. Kermit Sheets chose her to star in Shaw's *Candida*, leading to performances worthy to move to

San Francisco after the War, where many of the fine arts people joined the SF Renaissance movement. Ibby was under pressure to join in, but her commitment to me and our raising a large family prevailed. We had six children - one daughter, and five sons in ten years. Our family of four generations now numbers in the '40s and growing. In part, our need for family grows from the loss of Ibby's mother in an accident when Ibby was only three years old, as well as my having been raised in a large family.

In spite of living in the mid-west, we kept in touch with our dear Waldport friends through letters, phone calls, and reunion visits to California. We stayed with Kermit and his wife in several of their Marin County homes. We visited Bill Everson often, as well as Joyce and Adrian. Waldport influence and friends always remained at the center of our lives.

*I taught at Hanover College (Hanover, Indiana), Grinnell College (Grinnell, Iowa) and the University of Kansas (Laurence, Kansas) before creating an organization of behavioral scientists, the Midwest Group for Human Resources. We were part of the human potential movement during the '50s and '60s, based on the ethos of experimental learning. In 1970 I became President of the NT Institute of Applied Behavioral Science in Washington, D.C. In 1976 I left NTL to establish a private psychotherapy practice specializing in family therapy. I retired in 2002.*

*While living in Bethesda, MD, in the mid-1990s, my wife was diagnosed with Alzheimer's. We moved into a CCRC facility outside of Frederick, MD, which promised help. When it failed to help, we moved into a second CCRC in Grantville, MD, which provided excellent care for Ibby. In 1985 we purchased 16 acres of land near the headwaters of the Potomac River for which, in time, we created a land trust with the Maryland Environmental Trust to protect forever the butterflies which abounded there. This land, which we named Woodhill, remained very important to us until Ibby's death in 2007. Having retired from private practice in 2002, I lived there until my children convinced me, at age 90, to seek another CCRC. Like so many other residents of the University Retirement Community, my decision to move to Davis was based on having three children nearby. Since 2017, I have found a satisfactory end to my travels, finding URC a suitable new community.*

# The Home Front:
# The Japanese-American Experience

## Joyce Nao Takahashi

The year 1941 began with a lot of promise. In May, our family of four had taken a trip across the country from my birthplace, Berkeley, CA, to the East Coast to tour iconic places in American history, such as the Statue of Liberty and the Lincoln Memorial. I was bursting with patriotism for our country.

Then, on December 7, 1941, at about noon, our family heard the news that the Japanese had bombed the naval station at Pearl Harbor in Hawaii. My immediate reaction was one of anger at "those Japanese." "How dare they attack us!!," I thought. My Takahashi grandparents had come to the US at the turn of the century and had never returned to Japan. The rest of us were born here. I knew that we were Americans!! The farthest thought from my mind was that anyone would confuse our family with the enemy.

But I was mistaken, because on February 19, 1942, President Roosevelt issued EO 9066, which resulted in restrictions on everyone of Japanese ancestry who lived in Pacific Coast states. Everyone, whether alien or non-alien.

Finally, in April, my sister and I were coming home from school and read a notice tacked to a telephone post. It was Civilian Exclusion Order No. 19, which said that we were to be "excluded" from our home in Berkeley in one week. As head of the family, my father had to report that weekend to register "the family" including my grandparents, four of my five aunts and three uncles, the youngest of whom was a student at the University of California, Berkeley. We were identified as 13603A-M. We could take with us those personal items and pieces of clothing that we could carry, bedding and linen.

We were not charged with any crime or questioned about our loyalty.

Somehow, my parents arranged to rent out our house, sell the new car, close up my dad's optometry office, and pack our belongings. Before we left, Mildred Holmberg, who would live with her husband in our house for the next three years, sang "Bless This House."

We boarded the buses as the military stood erect holding their rifles. As we crossed the new Bay Bridge, I remembered the first time I had been on the bridge in 1939 going to the World's Fair on Treasure Island. We drove south of San Francisco on Hwy 101 and stopped at the grandstand of the Tanforan Race Track in San Bruno. Picture the area surrounded by barbed wire fencing with armed soldiers manning the guard towers and the gates. Inside, there would be about 8,000 internees from the Bay Area housed in the grandstand, tar paper barracks, and stables. Our family of four was assigned to a single horse/trainer stall next to the camp hospital, where my parents would work. The stall was 20 x 9 feet was divided into two sections by a swinging half-door. There were about 16 such units within each stable.

We slept on mattresses of straw-stuffed bags on top of army cots. Since there was no running water in the unit, we walked outside to the common latrines and washrooms.

Fellow internees cooked and dished up meals three times a day in mess halls. There were long lines for everything.

In the Fall of 1942, Tanforan Assembly Center was closed, and we were transported in lots of 500 by train to Topaz, Utah, nine miles northwest of Delta in the Sevier Desert. The one-mile square camp was surrounded by a barbed-wire fence and 7 guard towers and consisted of tar-papered barracks, which were arranged in an orderly grid along with the separate bath/laundry buildings and mess halls. This time we were assigned a 20' x 25' room. Our block #5 was next to the hospital where my parents worked for $19/month.

Topaz evolved into a community. After a few months, we still couldn't go home, but we could request "leave clearance" to join the army, to enroll in college, to accept a job somewhere. In January 1943, the US Army recruited 105 men from Topaz for the segregated 442nd Regimental Combat Team to fight on the European Front. Japanese-American men were already in the Military Intelligence Service, and they served as translators in the Pacific Front. Military stars appeared in barracks' windows.

In the spring of 1943, following the assault of one of our neighbors, our family received threatening notes, "you are next." Like the victim, my parents were considered "pro-American." We left. *(June 14, 1943)*. My father found a job with the Defense Department, my mother, with the Department of Public Health Nursing, and the extended family purchased a house in Chicago, Illinois. We returned to our home in Berkeley in the summer of 1945.

When three young men (Hirabayashi, Yasui, and Korematsu) defied the military orders and took their cases to the courts, the orders were upheld and the defendants were convicted in 1943-4. However, 40 years later, in 1983, the cases were reopened when it was discovered that the government had suppressed evidence. Their convictions were "vacated." Still later, each of the men was awarded a Presidential Medal of Freedom.

In 1988, a Congressional Commission determined that the treatment of the Japanese-Americans was caused by racial discrimination, wartime hysteria, and poor political leadership. A letter of apology was sent to all survivors by the President to each of us along with a $20,000 check.

Throughout our three-year exile from our home in Berkeley I cannot remember that my parents ever seemed upset about the indignity and injustice of the whole situation. In trying to understand how they could have done that, I recalled the 1998 Academy Award Italian film, "Life is Beautiful" in which Roberto Begnini protects his young son in a Nazi concentration camp by pretending that it is all a game. When I first saw the film, I did not like its slapstick humor, but now I see the film in a different light.

*Born in Berkeley, California, Joyce attended Longfellow Elementary, Burbank Junior High, Berkeley High and the University of California, Berkeley. She received her Ph. D. in Chemistry from the University of California, Los Angeles and lectured and conducted research principally at the University of California, Davis. She has two children.*

# My Father's War

## Judith Williams

My father Jim Newman had a hard life, but he was the most optimistic person I have ever known.

He had one semester of college education, despite having worked since he was 7 or 8 years old (initially running errands for a penny) to help support his mother and to save for college. He graduated from high school in 1929, and he started college that fall. When the banks closed after the stock market crash, he could not access the money he saved so he went back to work. My father worked all of his early life in the clothing business but took a job at Addressograph-Multigraph, a company that made equipment to make dog-tags, hoping to avoid the draft.

But in 1943, he was drafted despite being 32 years old and a father; my sister was born in February 1943.

My father went to Basic Training at Fort Hood in Texas. Most of the others drafted that year were recent high school graduates, and it was hard for him to keep up with the young recruits.

The stories he told my sister and me about his time at basic training were always meant to amuse. An example: When his unit was on bivouac, he was assigned to KP duty (after revealing the password to the other team while on guard duty). On KP, one of his jobs was serving breakfast. The men would step along in line and hold out their round mess kit for my father to put a healthy scoop of oatmeal on.

In the dim morning light, my father put that healthy scoop of oatmeal in the commanding officer's hat, not on his mess kit.

The story he never told us, but our mother did, was how he lost his right arm. Dad's unit was learning to shoot mortars. Mortars are small rockets aimed and launched by the troops. They have a sensitive tip which explodes on contact. The day my Dad's unit was to learn to launch mortars, the first 2 soldiers in line refused because they were certain that the way the equipment was set up, the mortar could brush the branches of an overhanging tree and explode over their heads. The drill sergeant sent them to the end of the line.

My father was one of the next 2 men in line. They knew nothing about the first 2 men, so they followed their orders, and exactly what the other men had predicted happened. My father's right arm was amputated in the field, the other soldier was also severely wounded, and the drill sergeant was killed. The Army evacuated my father to the Army hospital at Fort Bliss.

My mother received a telegram from the army informing her that my father had been wounded, but no further details. When she heard nothing further for many days and could not get in touch with anyone via telephone, she called the Red Cross. They were able to find him and told my mother where he was and what his condition was.

When my mother's father heard the news, he cried for my mother. He said, "Poor Jim. He won't even be able to wipe his ass for himself." The Veterans' Hospital proved my grandfather wrong. The physical and occupational therapy they gave my father was exceptional. Before long, my mother started to receive regular packages containing hand-tooled leather wallets, hand-tooled leather picture frames and belts, along with increasingly longer hand-written letters. (No one in our house was allowed to say anything negative about the Red Cross or the Veteran's Administration.)

My father told us stories about the hospital and the amputees at Fort Bliss. Those who had lost legs felt sorry for those who had lost arms and vice versa. When they got leave to go to town, the soldiers would get drunk and these two groups sometimes get into fights. The men who had lost a leg had an advantage if they could hop on their good foot and swing their crutches at the same time. My father always felt extremely sorry to hear that someone had lost their leg or their foot to diabetes.

My mother learned that you could send cookies though the mail packed in popcorn to protect them. My father wrote back thanking her for the popcorn, but asked her what those other crumbs were, though the system had actually worked quite well.

My father had always said that my mother made too big a deal about celebrating Christmas. He grew up so poor that Christmas was not much of a celebration. He usually got a pair of socks as his only gift. Christmas of 1944, he was in the hospital, when Bing Crosby introduced "I'll be home for Christmas." That song affected many GIs that year. My father thought it was the saddest song he could imagine. It ends with "I'll be home for Christmas if only in my dreams." But ever after, he was the one who went over the top on Christmas.

My uncle, who was in the Air Force and stationed in England, reportedly learned that my father's unit was completely wiped out in France.

When my father came home, it was as if he had not missed a beat. The only thing that he did not do is go back to the clothing business, and I think he always regretted that. Businessmen shook hands and clothiers measured inseams; he could not imagine how he could do this with only his left hand.

Instead he went back to Addressograph-Multigraph. The government required companies to find places for disabled vets when they came home. My father was a supervisor in the materials department. After the War, Addressograph changed their product from making dog-tags to making metal charge cards used by many department stores.

I was born in January 1945, 10 months after my father returned home. I know that a lot of what he had done before the War, like playing golf, changed for him (though he did play par 3 courses after he retired). He took up bowling.

One thing my father could not do was close the cuff links on his good hand. This was often my job, and I was proud to help him. He and his brother-in-law created devices for my father, such as a card rack and a cutting board with spikes to hold vegetables in place, so that he could lead a normal life.

Almost immediately after he returned home, he started a group called Opportunity Unlimited where he (and those he recruited) helped other amputees to learn some of the things the VA had taught him. Some of my earliest memories are of my dad sitting in the living room teaching guys how to tie their shoes or their neckties with one hand. In those days you didn't wear loafers to work, and anyone with a responsible job or a desire to go to church also wore a tie. The week my father died in his mid-80s, he had an appointment to meet with a young man who had lost a hand in a farm accident

To me having a father with one arm was not remarkable. Sometimes I went with him to have his prosthetic arm changed or adjusted. The amputation took his elbow, and there was no appliance that would give him any use of a hook or an artificial hand. As the years passed, however, he went from wearing a very heavy wooden arm with a brown leather glove on it to lighter plastic compounds and an artificial hand that looked realistic but did not do anything. The challenges were always with the straps that supported the arm which chaffed, or if incorrectly done, created terrible blisters or open wounds. It was also important to protect the stump. The field amputation had involved bundling up a bunch of ragged flesh and muscle, and sewing them around the jagged bone, all in unsanitary conditions. The stump was prone to infection, especially cellulitis which is fatal if not treated immediately. He developed scoliosis because of the weight of the arm. The day he retired he took off his arm and he never put it back on.

I learned some odd skills from my father. I learned that the easiest way to cut masking tape involved my teeth. The first time my husband asked me to dry dishes, I put a towel on the counter, and dabbed at a dish with a second towel. Prescott taught me an easier way to dry dishes.

President Truman gave us a brand new blue Oldsmobile 88 in about 1950. Or at least that is what I remember…

I NEVER heard my father complain. My sister and I knew that if we fell down and scraped our knees, or when my sister broke her nose, that we would get comfort from our folks. We also knew that these were small things, and we never expected nor asked for sympathy. We still don't.

*Judith and husband Prescott Williams moved to URC from Philadelphia in 2007. Judith Newman Williams grew up in Willoughby, Ohio. She and Prescott met at Gettysburg College. In 1966, the fall of her senior year, while Prescott was in Army Basic Training, they eloped and were married by the Justice of the Peace in Gettysburg. Prescott went on to earn an MEd in foreign language instruction at Rutgers, followed by*  *an MS in Technical Writing from Rensselaer Polytechnic Institute. The couple lived in Monterey, California, while Prescott studied Spanish at the Defense Language Institute before assignment in Puerto Rico. Judith began her career in education by teaching English at a parochial school near Bayamon, PR.*

*The Williamses have lived in southern New Jersey; Richmond, Virginia; Long Island, and Troy, New York before settling in Philadelphia. Judith taught English while earning her MS in Library Science. Judith retired in 2007 after working in public and private schools as a teacher, librarian, school administrator, and college counselor. They left Philadelphia to be closer to their daughter, Chesley. She and her husband Jake have raised two daughters while working as geologists. Chesley works in earthquake and tsunami risk assessment for a private company. Jake is a geochemist working for the US Geological Survey. For 15 years, he served as the geologist in charge of research at the Yellowstone Volcano Observatory.*

*Both Judith and Prescott have been busy in their retirement, volunteering both in Davis and at URC. Both have worked on and chaired committees, and both have served as President of the Resident Council. Judith has worked on the Resident Foundation Committee and is an* URCADIAN *editor.*

# Acknowledgments

The inspiration for this book came to your Editor upon his arrival as a resident of the University Retirement Community in Davis, California. Early on, I became aware of a display in the main building entrance of a panel of photographs of people in uniform which was part of a Veteran's Day observance, an annual event at URC. Later, as a member of the Inreach/Outreach Committee, I asked if any thought had been given to publishing a book honoring those who had served in World War II and were residents of our facility. Previously there had been collections of personal accounts of war experience, but these writings had never been collected in an actual book.

At the suggestion of the committee chairperson Georgia Paulo, the committee voted to request funding for such an endeavor as a worthy project. As a result of the request, an amount to cover the initial publication cost was approved and work began gathering material for the book.

The format chosen was patterned on publications by other CCRC's that had published similar collections. The resources that were available varied from previously written stories to interviews with veterans and others who had stories to tell of their experiences during the War. With the advanced ages of participants, we were anxious to include every resident who qualified as having served in the military during that period and others who had kept the home fires burning. In the case of stories written by the participants themselves, we determined that the histories be in their own words wherever possible. In the case of interviews, they were all transcribed into first-person accounts. It was also our intention to also include residents who did not serve in the military but had memories of helping in the war effort. In addition to several residents born overseas, we included experiences of Japanese-Americans who were relocated to camps early after Pearl Harbor, some for the duration of the conflict. We also felt it important to share the experience of a conscientious objector to round out the range of experiences related to the War.

This book would not have been possible without the help of our contributing editors who collected the materials, who conducted the interviews, submitted other materials and helped generate them for the book including Joan Callaway, Lena McNicholas, Amy Moore, Georgia Paulo Jasper Schad, Joyce Takahashi and Prescott Williams. Also, invaluable services were performed by Judy Wydich in proofreading and Ray Vincent, who contributed many of the World War II era photographs. Last, and certainly not least, was the diligent and critical work of laying out the final publication performed by resident Scott Johnson.

Funding for the publication of the book came from a grant from the University Retirement Community and its Executive Director Alika Castillo. The final product would not have been possible without the expertise and hard work of our publisher's Gerald Ward of the *I Street Press* of the Sacramento Public Library. And, for the many residents who contributed in other ways, this is your book.